A Symposium on Scriptural Holiness

Edited by
Rev. Wilson T. Hogg

*President of Greenville College,
and Editor of
"The Free Methodist"*

"Be Ye Holy."

Schmul Publishing Company
Nicholasville, Kentucky

COPYRIGHT © 2016 BY SCHMUL PUBLISHING CO.
All rights reserved. No part of this publication may be reproduced or used in any form or by any means—graphic, electronic, or mechanical, including photocopying, recording, taping, or information storage or retrieval systems—without prior written permission of the publishers.

Churches and other noncommercial interests may reproduce portions of this book without prior written permission of the publisher, provided such quotations are not offered for sale—or other compensation in any form—whether alone or as part of another publication, and provided that the text does not exceed 500 words or five percent of the entire book, whichever is less, and does not include material quoted from another publisher. When reproducing text from this book, the following credit line must be included: "From *A Symposium on Scriptural Holiness*, Ed. by Wilson T. Hogg, © 2016 by Schmul Publishing Co., Nicholasville, Kentucky. Used by permission."

Published by Schmul Publishing Co.
PO Box 776
Nicholasville, KY USA

Printed in the United States of America

ISBN 10: 0-88019-595-9
ISBN 13: 978-0-88019-595-9

Visit us on the Internet at www.wesleyanbooks.com, or order direct from the publisher by calling 800-772-6657, or by writing to the above address.

Contents

	Editor's Preface 5	
1	Holiness not Understood 9	
	Rev. Benjamin Titus Roberts, A. M.	
2	Holiness the Main Theme of the Bible 15	
	Rev. Edward Payson Hart	
3	The Nature of Scriptural Holiness 19	
	Rev. George Whitefield Coleman	
4	Legal and Evangelical Holiness Contrasted 25	
	Rev. Levi Wood	
5	Holiness Attainable in the Present Life 31	
	Rev. Walter A. Sellew, A. M.	
6	Holiness a Privilege 36	
	Rev. Charles B. Ebey	
7	Holiness a Necessity 41	
	Rev. Burton Rensselaer Jones	
8	Holiness as Related to Justification and Sanctification 47	
	Rev. Charles M. Damon	
9	Conviction for Holiness 51	
	Rev. A.J. M'Kinney	
10	Consecration and Holiness 56	
	Rev. Moses N. Downing	
11	The Revelation of Faith to Holiness 60	
	Rev. Wilson T. Hogg	

12	FRUITS OF HOLINESS 65
	Rev. W.B. Olmstead
13	PROFESSING HOLINESS 69
	Benson Howard Roberts, A.M.
14	RETAINING HOLINESS 73
	Mrs. Emma Sellew Roberts, A.M.
15	HOLINESS AS A STATE OF CHRISTIAN PERFECTION 78
	Rev. Duane C. Johnson
16	PERFECTING HOLINESS 83
	Rev. Wilson T. Hogg
17	HOLINESS AND THE MINISTRY 87
	Rev. Wilson T. Hogg
18	HOLINESS THE POWER OF THE CHURCH 92
	Rev. F.D. Brooke
19	PREACHING HOLINESS 97
	Rev. John La Due
20	MEETINGS FOR HOLINESS 101
	Mrs. M.H. Freeland
21	HOLINESS AND REFORMS 104
	Rev. Charles H. Rawson, A.M.
22	PRACTICAL HOLINESS 111
	Mrs. Mary C. Baker
23	SPURIOUS HOLINESS 116
	Rev. J.T. Logan
24	ADVICE TO THOSE PROFESSING HOLINESS 124
	Albert H. Stilwell, A.M.
	HOLINESS AT DEATH 128
	Rev. S. K. Wheatlake
	OUT AND INTO 133
	THE MASTER'S TOUCH 135

Editor's Preface

If any apology is needed for sending out this little volume we have one and only one to offer, namely, an earnest desire to add, so far as possible, to the agencies already at work for spreading Scriptural holiness over the land.

The articles herein contained, with two exceptions, were originally prepared for a special Holiness issue of the *Free Methodist* which appeared March 4, 1896. When received they were considered too good to be allowed to disappear with the weekly issue of the paper which contained them, and so it was decided between the editor and publisher to electrotype the matter and put it into a more permanent form than that of a mere newspaper publication. Whether this was wise or otherwise the patronage the work receives will help us to determine.

If there shall be found some repetition in the work, let it be remembered that each writer wrote without knowing what other topics were to be discussed, in which case it was scarcely possible for all repetition to be avoided. We have been surprised, however, that the repetitions are so few, and we are more than pleased that there are no conflicting views expressed by the twenty-one different writers who have contributed this series of papers on Scriptural holiness.

The first paper in the series is from the able pen of the late Rev. B.T. Roberts, and is reprinted from the *Earnest Christian*, by permission, as a most suitable leader to the series which follows it. The paper on "Perfecting Holiness" is part of a sermon preached at the International Holiness Convention held in Chicago several years ago, and which was published in the report of that convention. The other articles have been specially prepared for the Symposium, and so have the quality of freshness, at least.

We now send forth this little volume in the divine Master's name and with the hope and prayer that his blessing may so attend it as to make it in some measure effective in hastening the day when "*Holiness unto the Lord* shall be written upon the bells of the horses", and when "the earth shall be filled with the knowledge of the glory of the Lord, as the waters cover the sea."

REV. BENJAMIN TITUS ROBERTS

1
HOLINESS NOT UNDERSTOOD

THE BIBLE HAS MUCH TO SAY about holiness. It is an attribute of God (Psa. 60:6; Rev. 4:8, *et al*). We are commanded to follow it (Heb. 12:14); to worship God in the beauty of holiness (Psa. 29:2). Without it we cannot see the Lord (Heb. 12:14). It is the one thing needful. There are many things which are convenient and useful; but this alone is indispensable to our welfare both in this world and in the world to come. It is important, then, that we have correct ideas of its nature. If we would hit a mark we must know where to aim. If we would attain an excellence we must know what it is. He who would search for diamonds, must know diamonds when he finds them.

Upon first view, it may seem that men are pretty well agreed as to what constitutes holiness; but, on reflection, this will be seen to be a mistake. Upon this point there is a wide diversity of opinion. Such is the imperfection of language and such the constitution of particular minds that the same words often fail to express the same idea to different persons, even when they are equally candid. But take holiness in its most tangible form— take it as exemplified in the lives of holy persons— and it is not generally acknowledged to be holiness. It is usually called by almost any other name than holiness. In God's sight, Job was a holy person. He said, "Hast thou considered my servant Job, that there is none like him in the earth, a perfect and an upright man, one that feareth God and escheweth evil" (Job 1:8)? But even his friends labored to convince him that he was a wicked man. Eliphaz says to him, "They that plough iniquity and sow wickedness, reap the same" (Job 4:8). Bildad takes up the accusation and reminds him that "The hypocrite's hope shall perish" (Job 8:13). Zophar asks him, "Should thy lies make men hold their peace" (Job 11:3)? And even Elihu exclaims, "What man is like Job, who drinketh up scorning like water? Which goeth in company with the workers of iniquity, and walketh with wicked men" (Job 34:7,8)? This was the opinion which his friends had of him, as expressed to his face. Of course the judgment of his enemies was much more unfavorable.

Our Saviour exemplified holiness in its most perfect form. In his life, his conversation, his spirit, and in all his actions he was holiness personified. He gave the most unmistakable proofs of disinterested love to all mankind. Yet the popular verdict concerning him was, "Behold a man gluttonous, and a wine bibber, a friend of publicans and sinners" (Matt. 11:19).

Christ told his disciples that they must not expect to be appreciated any better than he was. "If they have called the master of the house Beelzebub, how much more shall they call them of his household" (Matt. 10:25)? From that day down to the present, holiness in the disciples of Christ has been recognized by but few, even of those who call themselves Christians. John Wesley stated clearly, defended ably, and exemplified in his life the doctrine of holiness. Whitefield for burning zeal, and simple devotion to the cause of Christ, has not had a superior since the days of St.

Paul. Yet the Rev. Sydney Smith, a clergyman of the same church as that to which Wesley and Whitefield belonged, a writer of great celebrity, but expressed the estimate in which they were held by their fellow clergymen, when he said: "They were men of considerable talent; they observed the common decorums of life; they did not run naked into the streets or pretend to be prophetical characters;— and therefore they were not committed to Newgate. They preached with great energy to weak people, who first stared, then listened— then believed— then felt the inward feeling of grace, and became as foolish as their teachers could possibly wish them to be; in short folly ran its ancient course;— and human nature evinced itself to be what it always has been, under similar circumstances. The great and permanent cause, therefore, of Methodism, is the cause winch has given birth to fanaticism in all ages— the facility of mingling human errors with the fundamental truths of religion."

In our day we see that which we deem essential to holiness purposely omitted in instructions upon this subject. Popular sins, are, to say the least, silently tolerated. During the war of the rebellion, in a popular meeting for the promotion of holiness, in the city of New York, Brother D. F. Newton thanked the Lord for President Lincoln's Emancipation Proclamation. He was at once called to order for introducing a topic calculated to disturb the harmony of the meeting. There are many works on the subject of holiness, written in the days of slave-holding to circulate among slave-holders, and not a word to be found in them condemning the practice. The same spirit which led to silence respecting slave-holding in the days when all the popular churches welcomed the slave-holders to their communion, to-day utterly ignores the existence of sins which God's word plainly condemns, but which the leading churches openly tolerate. That which encourages what God forbids is not holiness. The name of a thing does not give it its nature.

There is a powerful secret society, spreading itself throughout the country, composed largely of unbelievers, to which, however, many ministers and church members belong. This society is thoroughly anti-Christian in its character. To pray in the lodge in the name of Christ is declared by the highest Masonic authority to be a violation of the fundamental principles of Masonry. The members bind themselves by the most horrid oaths to submit to be murdered, and to conceal, and even commit murder under certain circumstances. Of these facts any intelligent person can easily satisfy himself beyond the shadow of a doubt. Yet in many meetings held for the promotion of holiness, to point out these hindrances to the work of holiness would be considered impertinent and fanatical.

Again, the persecution to which the saints of God have always been subjected, shows that holiness is not recognized when seen. The word declares, "Yea, and all that will live godly in Christ Jesus shall suffer persecution" (2 Tim. 3:12). This persecution varies in its form with the prevailing spirit of the age. But whatever shape it assumes, persecution never assigns as its reason, the godliness of its victims. Their obstinacy, or contumacy, or disloyalty, or heresy is assigned as the cause of their sufferings. Christ was put to death as an impostor. Luther was excommunicated as a heretic, and Wesley and Whitefield were hunted as fanatics. Their persecutors were the professed children of God, and they believed it to be a zeal for holiness which instigated their opposition to those who furnished bright examples of holiness in their lives.

On the other hand, there are those who make holiness comprise attributes which are entirely beyond the reach of a human being in our present condition. They give a meaning to the term which the scriptures do not warrant. According to their standard, a holy person cannot make a mistake in judgment, either through ignorance or misapprehension. He must not only do right, as he understands it, but do right as they understand it, under all circumstances. They measure others by their own infallibility. They make no allowances for lack of judgment or for imperfect training. He who professes holiness, must be, according to their views, beyond the reach of unfriendly criticism. In addition to all this, he must never fall. Should he ever afterward manifest any disposition contrary to his profession, it is then assumed that all along he was either deceived or hypocritical. If he lost holiness, the conclusion is not only that he never had holiness, but that no one ever did or ever will. In short, holiness is pronounced unattainable because some who appeared once to have attained it did not persevere to the end.

Thus a false standard of holiness is raised, and then holiness is declared to be an impossibility, because no one is found to come up to this imaginary standard. We are told to aim our arrow at the sun, and then are ridiculed because we fall short of the mark. The moral perfections of God are presented as our standard, and then we are gravely told that we cannot attain it.

Rev. Benjamin Titus Roberts, A. M.,
Founder and first Superintendent of the Free Methodist Church

Rev. Edward Payson Hart

2
HOLINESS THE MAIN THEME OF THE BIBLE

"ALL ROADS LEAD to Rome." As certainly as Rome was the great center and head of the empire of the Caesars, so is "Holiness the main theme of the Bible." Take up whatever phase of Bible teaching we may, whether historical, geographical, typical or experimental, all lead to and end at the one point of moral purity. "In the beginning God created the heaven and the earth" is but the history of the formation of a planet to be peopled by a new order of intelligences patterned after the moral image of Deity. All through the first chapter of Genesis we read that God [*Elohim*] "created," "called," "said" and "set". But in the second chapter, just preceding the account of man's shameful sin and fall— as if overshadowing mercy were already preparing a hiding-place from wrath— another person of the Godhead appears and we read, "The Lord God [*Yahveh Elohim*] said," etc. Follow the history on down and you come to the Jesus of the New Testament— the Yahveh or Jehovah of the Old. New Testament history treats of the advent, the three years' ministry, the temptation, the wrestling, the sacrificial death and glorious resurrection of the Son of God. In the account of his death we are told, "But one of the soldiers with a spear pierced his side, and forthwith came there out blood and water." The real significance of this is brought out by Mr. Toplady in a verse of that beautiful hymn—

"Rock of ages, cleft for me,
Let me hide myself in thee;
Let the water and the blood,
From thy wounded side which flowed,
Be of sin the double cure,—
Save from wrath, and make me pure."

The geography of the Bible is but a description of those parts of the earth's surface where, either in triumph or in humiliation, lived the people through whom the purposes of God, in the great work of human redemption, were to be wrought out,— until, overleaping the boundaries of this present world, it speaks of the earth purified by fire and peopled with a race redeemed by blood; and John, wrapped in apocalyptic vision, viewing the scene, cries, "And I saw a new heaven and a new earth: for the first heaven and the first earth were passed away; and there was no more sea. And I John saw the holy city, new Jerusalem, coming down from God out of heaven, prepared as a bride adorned for her husband. And I heard a great voice out of heaven saying, Behold, the tabernacle of God is with men, and he will dwell with them, and they shall be his people, and God himself shall be with them, and be their God. And God shall wipe away all tears from their eyes; and there shall be no more death, neither sorrow, nor crying, neither shall there be anymore pain: for the former things are passed away" (Rev. 21:1-4).

In the Bible we have not only a law given as a code of morals, but also what is termed the ceremonial law— a law of types and shadows. As young children, by the use of pictures and object lessons, are taught to read, so the Lord by the types and shadows of this law endeavored to educate the mind of humanity up to the conception and apprehension of separation from moral defilement and cleansing from moral pollution. How clearly and how beautifully Paul, in the tenth chapter of his epistle to the Hebrews, shows that this law being but "the shadow of good things to come," is ineffectual by its sacrifices to take away sin; and further shows how unerringly these oft-repeated sacrifices point to the offering once for all of the body of Christ, which offering alone is efficacious for perfect remission and cleansing!

The prophetical scriptures form no small and no unimportant part of the sacred word. How, like the search-light of God, prophecy shines down through the mist of the ages and reveals the Son of man! With what precision it discloses beforehand events which have now passed into history! In its light kings pass away, thrones crumble, and kingdoms decay. But it also reveals a King who shall reign in righteousness," "whose kingdom shall be an everlasting kingdom," and whose throne shall stand eternally. It speaks of the sprinkling of clean water that shall make clean— of the "fountain opened… for sin and uncleanness". Neither can the spiritual application of these prophecies be questioned, for it was the Spirit of Christ in the holy men of old which signified, and testified beforehand these very things. Moreover, we are plainly told that "The testimony of Jesus is the spirit of prophecy"; and without doing violence to the text we may transpose and read *"The spirit of prophecy is the testimony of Jesus"*.

To undertake to show that the experimental teaching of the Bible leads directly to holiness would be to quote a large proportion of the holy word. We are told time and again of the provision made for the attainment of this experience. We are repeatedly invited and urged to the attainment of it; we are called with a holy calling;" and, finally, we are under the express command of God concerning it.

So apparent is it that holiness is the main theme of this blessed book that all civilized and Christian people unite in stamping it with the title, "Holy Bible".

REV. EDWARD PAYSON HART,
Senior General Superintendent of the Free Methodist Church

3
THE NATURE OF SCRIPTURAL HOLINESS

BEFORE ENTERING DIRECTLY upon a consideration of the subject, it may be proper to state that there is *no other kind* of holiness. If the term holiness had never been misapplied or fraudulently applied in order to make unholy things seem holy, no qualifying term would be needed. To apply the term to anything that tolerates sin or that has affinity with evil of any kind, however, is to use it as a misnomer.

All true holiness in the universe has come from God. No creature ever possessed any but what was derived from him. Hence wherever found — in angels or men — it is composed of the same qualities. It is, like God himself, unchangeable. He alone can impart it to others. No creature, though possessed of it himself, can convey it to another. He can only direct the attention of another to the source of supply. God has been putting it within the hearts of the intelligent beings he has made, and bestowing it on every converted soul from the beginning; and yet the same infinite supply is with him as at first. Our natural sun is constantly giving off light and heat to a degree that passes human comprehension; and yet after thousands of years it

Rev. George Whitefield Coleman

shines with the same undiminished splendor as at first. What feeds its perpetual fires is beyond the power of human ken to apprehend. The glorious "Sun of righteousness" will never exhaust the supply of spiritual light and heat essential to the life of holiness in the human soul.

The nature of scriptural holiness is precisely the same as the nature and character of God. The character of any being is produced by the moral nature he possesses, and the two always have the same moral complexion. Holiness, then, is likeness to God in moral nature and character. The Bible calls it "godliness." When God made man he said, "Let us make man in our image, after our likeness." Every child of God is a "partaker of the divine nature" — "partaker of his holiness." It is the highest quality in the divine Being, and the greatest boon he has to confer on his creatures. It not only produces the best type of character possible, but the only one in which true happiness is to be found. It is the supreme quality in the bosom of the Almighty, and in the hearts of all his children.

Holiness is so much a part of God that we cannot think of him aright without including it. His natural attributes are wonderful and glorious, and surpass human thought; but his holiness eclipses them all. There is no moral quality necessarily in any of them; though they are all essential qualities of the divine character. Omnipotence, omniscience, omnipresence, immutability, eternity, are all essential attributes of divinity, but without holiness to direct in the use of them, God were better off without them. We may admire the exhibition of his power, wisdom, unchangeableness, his immortality and ability to be everywhere present, without dwelling on his holiness; but if we have true love for him, it is because of the beauty of his character, which is described as "glorious in holiness." Nor can this ever take place until we have "put on Christ", and hence become able to love what he loves and hate what he hates.

Holiness has both a positive and a negative side. Holiness in God is that disposition or quality that gives him an infinite love for all that is right, and pure, and good, and an infinite abhorrence for all that is evil and unrighteous. It produces the same affections and feelings in finite beings, in their measure, that it does in the Almighty. We always find in a holy person an aversion for that which is impure and sinful. "Ye that fear the Lord, hate evil." The measure of our hatred for that which is opposed to God indicates the intensity of our love for that which pleases him. Holiness is an active principle, and always stimulates its possessor to do all in his power to secure in others the same blessed experience. It produces in finite beings, in their measure, like feelings for the welfare of their fellows to that which moved our heavenly Father to provide salvation for the human family.

Wherever holiness exists it actuates, dominates and controls the person. Hence, every Christian has his "fruit unto holiness and the end everlasting life." Holiness will never go into partnership with what is unlike itself. If we desire holiness, before we can get it we shall have to abandon sin in all its forms and phases, and separate ourselves from sinners, except so far as duty requires us to mingle with them. "Wherefore come out from among them, and be ye separate, and touch not the unclean thing." Holiness will never abide in the heart longer than it continues to be a perfectly welcome guest. It is too valuable a boon to be lavished on unappreciative hearts. Only those who have freely given *all* to obtain it would give it suitable attention if received. The Bible says, "Give not that which is holy unto the dogs, neither cast ye your pearls before swine, lest they trample them under their feet, and turn again and rend you" (Matt 7:6).

Love, as applied to God, is synonymous with the word holiness, or at least very nearly so. It is more likely, however, to confuse the ordinary mind, because we so commonly associate it with the same word as expressing natural affection. The two words in the original are entirely unlike. One is *philos,* meaning human love; and the other *agape,* referring to divine love. These two words, both translated "love" in our version, are entirely unlike in their deeper signification, although they have this in common, they are both affections of the heart and they act spontaneously where they exist. Love is numbered among the graces of the spirit, but is often used as inclusive of them all. "God is love." Watts exclaims, —

> "My passions hold a pleasing reign,
> When love inspires my breast;
> Love, the divinest of the train,
> The sovereign of the rest."

As love is often used to include all of the Christian graces, so holiness includes all the moral excellencies of Deity.

Righteousness is not exactly synonymous with holiness, though they are nearly akin to each other in signification, and are sometimes used interchangeably. Holiness refers more especially to the state, or moral condition of the person, while righteousness applies more appropriately to the acts performed. One who is holy in heart will always be righteous in life. The apostle uses these terms to describe the whole image of God, "And that ye put on the new man, which after God is created in righteousness and true holiness" (Eph. 4:24).

Holiness is of such a nature that it may be possessed in different degrees. The lowest degree, however, will break the power and deliver from the dominion of sin. "For sin shall not have dominion over you" (Rom. 6:14). Entire holiness, or "perfect love", eradicates the very inbeing of sin. "The blood of Jesus Christ cleanseth us from all sin" (I John 1:7). The work of holiness is begun in justifying grace; it is completed, so far as the destruction of all that is opposed to God in us is concerned, when we are entirely sanctified.

By the light of holiness received when converted we discover the need of inward purity and the will of God in its bestowment. When cleansed from all unrighteousness and filled with the perfect love of God all inclination to sin and proneness to wander will be gone. Still the vessel may be enlarged and repeatedly filled. The process of development in divine things will go on unobstructed forever.

Rev. George Whitefield Coleman,
General Superintendent of the Free Methodist Church

4
LEGAL AND EVANGELICAL HOLINESS CONTRASTED

THE WORD HOLY, used only as an adjective, is in the New Testament in one hundred and seventy-five places. In eighty-six of these places it occurs in the phrase "Holy Ghost." In four places it is in the phrase "Holy Spirit." The words "ghost" and "spirit" are from the same word in the Greek, namely, *pneuma*. In each of these ninety places the absolute holiness of the third person of the Holy Trinity is denoted. In John 17:11 the word holy is applied to the first person of the Trinity— "*holy* Father." In eight places the word is applied to the incarnated second person of the Trinity— our Lord Jesus Christ. The word in all such connections comprehends full or entire holiness. In four places it applies to the angels in the phrase, "holy angels"; here also it implies complete holiness. Four times it is used in a full sense in the phrase "Holy Scriptures," or words equivalent. In thirty places the word holy is applied to things, places, or actions: these may be complete or incomplete in holiness, which must be determined by the connection and circumstances of the case.

In nearly all the other places in the New Testament where the adjective holy occurs it applies to human beings in some form. These are to be regarded as complete or incomplete in holiness according as they have attained to a complete deliverance from all inherent sin or not.

There are two words in the original very different from each other, both which we translate holy. The one, *hosios*, means properly *merciful*. This occurs but six times. The other, *hagios*, which is found in the Greek New Testament one hundred and sixty-seven times, implies much more. It properly means *separated*— "separated from sin." When God is called holy, it means that he is separate from all moral and natural evil, and from all created beings and things. So of a human soul; it is entirely holy when sin is all separated from it, so that it can love God supremely, every other feeling being subservient to this.

The term holiness occurs twelve times in the New Testament. Its full meaning is deliverance from all sin, outward and inward, and implies a pure heart (Matt. 5:8).

Man in his natural state is a perfect negation— no holiness. "For I know that in me (that is, in my flesh) dwelleth no good thing" (Rom. 7:18).

Man completely saved from sin is in an entirely positive state. "They were all filled with the Holy Ghost" (Acts 2:4). "Filled with all the fulness of God" (Eph. 3:19).

Now the transition from no holiness to complete holiness is not to be realized in an instant. God grades all his works. It takes time to pass from midnight to noon. In the creation each day's work showed progress, a getting nearer to the final completeness. In the temple was first, the outer court; second, the holy place; third, the holy of holies. Birth, babyhood, childhood, youth, manhood; the patriarchal age, the Jewish age, the Christian age, the millennium, and then final and eternal glory. In Ezekiel's vision of the holy waters the waters rose first to the ankles, then to the knees, then to the loins, and then they became "a mighty river, waters to swim in, a river which could not be passed over." There are grades in Christian experience. Vile man, utterly fallen, cannot leap into entire holiness at a single bound. "They go from strength to strength in Zion."

Notice some of the steps taken as a soul makes progress from its Adamic or natural state toward the fulness to be found in Christ. Awakening, conviction, repentance, confession, saving faith, pardon, regenerating grace— or the implanting of the seed or principle of eternal life in the soul, adoption, assurance or the witness of the Spirit, victory over those peculiar temptations incident to early experience; and then later on, covering more or less time as God ordains, comes a sense of inward impurity, a feeling of want, a longing to become wholly Christlike, an inward struggle of soul to conquer inward sin, the exercise of the faith which brings the uttermost salvation, the inward cleansing, the full baptism of the Spirit, the inward witness of full salvation, victory over those strong temptations incident to the earlier stages of entire sanctification; and then, finally, a fixedness of the soul in the enjoyment of all those blessings which belong to full salvation. Here is Jacob's ladder with twenty rounds, from the top round of which the entirely sanctified soul steps off into Paradise as it leaves the present life for the eternal life beyond.

Although these are the prime steps taken, yet in the Christian life are two principal epochs of experience. The first is known as conversion, the second as entire sanctification. At conversion the soul experiences pardon, the impartation of spiritual life, adoption, and assurance, with love, joy and peace. Although these are to be thought of in the order here stated, yet they seem to come into the soul all at once in a flood of salvation, and there is no perceptible difference of time. And for a season, longer or shorter, the soul is absorbed in its new experiences, and remains unconscious of its remaining inherent depravity. Then, if the soul has been faithful, there comes a realization of the need of a deeper experience, even a conviction for, and, if properly sought, the experience of full salvation.

The phrase "sanctify you wholly" in 1 Thess. 5:23, implies such a thing as a partial sanctification— this the newly justified soul has: now if he would be sanctified wholly he must walk in the light and be led of the Spirit until he attains unto that full redemption which is to be found by faith in the blood of the Lamb. We refer the reader to another text: "And I, brethren, could not speak unto you as unto spiritual, but as unto carnal, even as unto babes in Christ (1 Cor. 3: 1). This verse with its context shows us clearly that a "babe in Christ" is still to some extent carnal— it takes full salvation, experienced later on, to get all carnality, all inward sinfulness out of the heart.

This full salvation, or holiness completed in the soul, is wholly the product of the Holy Spirit. No man can make himself holy, no, not even measureably so. What may be termed legal holiness, or holiness by law, is purely a human product, and is entirely worthless. It consists in an effort to keep the law in our own strength, and is therefore simply Pharisaism. It strikes root in carnal self, and is the effort of a sinner to make himself his own Savior. It has a form of godliness, but knows absolutely nothing of the power and blessedness of true religion. It sometimes tries hard in an outward, sanctimonious way to keep the whole law, while it remains as graceless as the whistling wind, and as groundless as "the baseless fabric of a vision." It has a ritualism, ordinances and forms of service of which it is very tenacious, and seems to proceed on the supposition that outward activity and an outward conformity to the letter of the law are the very essence of the religion of Jesus. The apostle labels this kind of holiness thus— "my own righteousness, which is of the law" (Phil. 3:9). That was the kind of holiness he had while he was Saul of Tarsus, and a carping Pharisee. It goes without saying, that very much of the religion of the present age savors very strongly of this spurious kind.

Evangelical holiness, on the other hand, strikes root in Christ, and is the product of saving grace in the soul. This is the work of God: the other is the work of man. Evangelical holiness is to be contradistinguished from and contrasted with legal holiness very much as we would contrast day with night, life with death, sanity with insanity, or a living, healthy man with an automaton. The apostle puts his label on true holiness thus— "that which is through the faith of Christ, the righteousness which is of God by faith" (Phil. 3:9).

Evangelical holiness, which is a result of saving faith in the infinite merits of Christ, is a divine, up-lifting power, which lifts the soul up into God, and heaven, and everlasting life. Conversely, a legal holiness— an effort to obtain justification and full righteousness by obedience to law— will but prove a dead weight to the soul to sink it down into the fathomless depths of eternal despair. The voice of Revelation to fallen, depraved man is not, "Do, and live"; but, "BELIEVE, and BE SAVED."

But does not a holy soul keep the holy law of God? He certainly does; but not in his own strength. Jesus says, "Without me ye can do nothing." It is only as we have Christ formed within us, the hope of eternal glory, that we are able through him to render all obedience to law, both in the letter and spirit of it. It is grace that triumphs over sin, not nature. The righteousness of the law is fulfilled *in* and *by* them who walk not after the flesh, but after the Spirit. (See Rom. 8:4.)

Reader, beware of the influence of those whose religion is mere form and ceremony without any semblance of spiritual life. If the Holy Ghost is not in the service, regard it not, be not conformed to it, seek better associations and a better religion. "The letter killeth, but the Spirit giveth life." "To him who worketh not, but believeth on him who justifieth the ungodly, his faith is counted for righteousness" (Rom. 4:5). "By grace are ye saved, through faith; and that not of yourselves; it [the salvation] is the gift of God" (Eph. 2:8). "It is the Spirit that quickeneth; the flesh profiteth nothing."

Rev. Levi Wood,
Original Proprietor and Editor of the Free Methodist

5
HOLINESS ATTAINABLE IN THE PRESENT LIFE

No intelligent religionist has ever yet asserted or assumed that anything unholy could enter heaven. It is agreed on every side that all who are eternally saved must be holy some time. The question at issue is, therefore, wholly one of time.

Opinion divides us into three classes on this subject: Those who believe we are made holy (*a*) in this present life, (*b*) at death, and (*c*) after death.

The theory of entire sanctification as necessarily postponed until death is losing its place in theology; and, while it remains in the creed of a large number of believers, comparatively few are to be found who really believe it. The issue is being drawn more and more clearly between entire sanctification in this life and entire sanctification after death (future probation), which is essentially the same as universalism.

There are three sources at least on which we may draw for arguments on this subject. These are reason, revelation and experience.

There are some considerations on account of which it would appear *reasonable*, at least, that God should make us holy in this present life.

1. In such a state we could serve him better. The relations naturally existing between us and God would teach us that his people should serve him faithfully all their days. Sin is a hideous moral leprosy. Passing the question whether any acceptable service is possible while sin remains in the heart, it must be admitted that sin is a most serious hindrance to our spiritual service. Holiness would wonderfully increase both the extent and value of that service, as well as the enjoyment of the person rendering it. How could God arrange for sin to remain in us all our lives? What good can possibly result from such a condition? What incalculable evil and misery must result from it instead!

2. All ideals are based upon perfection. The artist, the architect, the mechanic, and all whose lives have anything whatever of aspiration connected with them, strive after perfection. Anything short of it brings criticism, partial or total failure, and frequently ruin, disgrace and misery. Such failures frequently turn mortals from the earthly to the heavenly, from the material to the spiritual. Is it reasonable that God would put into the soul of man an ideal of love and loyalty to him and then constitute an environment of impossibility? It is contrary to reason to struggle for the impossible.

3. No other moral standard of life is possible. It is either entire holiness or unmitigated confusion. All who deny holiness to be a possibility in this life admit that we should strive after it with all our powers. If we cannot obtain what we strive after, who shall decide how much less than entire sanctification is allowable? If some sin can be tolerated, who shall decide how much? If we may be delivered from some sin, why not from still more? If we can be rid of nearly all sin, why not of all? If not of all, shall it be left to some denomination of believers, or to some society, or to a committee, or to each individual, to determine how much sin is allowable; to draw the line between the possible and the impossible?

4. If holiness can be attained after death, it would cause our efforts towards its attainment to weaken if not entirely cease. There would be a more or less gradual, but a certain settling down to a life of self-indulgence. If it is asserted that none can be made holy after death who do not strive for it here, it may be answered: Who shall determine how much striving here is necessary to entitle one to the benefits of future probation?

5. Entire sanctification or holiness here, and that alone, answers all objections, satisfies all demands, reaches all ideals and produces satisfactory results. If God is able to make us holy here, it would seem unreasonable that he should be unwilling to do so. If he is both able and willing, how much more unreasonable that it should not be done!

When we turn from reason to *Revelation* we are embarrassed at the wealth of scripture at our command. Instead of having to rely on one or two passages of doubtful application, we have so many which are clear and plain, that it would seem they only needed to be read to convince anyone that entire sanctification is for this life.

1. It is God's will that we should be holy here, even in our bodies. If our bodies are holy by the indwelling of a holy soul, it must be in this life. "For God has not called us unto uncleanness, but unto holiness" (1 Thes. 4:7; also read Rom. 12:1, 2; and 1 Thes. 4:1, 3).

2. Jesus and inspired writers, either for themselves or for others, prayed for holiness as an experience here. "Sanctify them through thy truth: thy word is truth… And for their sakes I sanctify myself, that they also might be sanctified through the truth" (John 17:17-19). "Wash me thoroughly from mine iniquity, and cleanse me from my sin." "Create in me a clean heart, O God; and renew a right spirit within me" (Psa. 51:2, 10). "The very God of peace sanctify you wholly; and I pray God your whole spirit and soul and body be preserved blameless unto the coming of

our Lord Jesus Christ. Faithful is he that calleth you, who also will do it" (1 Thes. 5:23,24).

3. The word of God encourages and urges us towards holiness as a present experience. "Therefore leaving the principles of the doctrine of Christ, let us go on unto perfection" (Heb. 6:1). "I will walk within my house with a perfect heart" (Psa. 101:2). "Truly God is good to Israel, even to such as are of a clean heart" (Psa. 73:1). "There is no fear in love; but perfect love casteth out fear" (1 John 4:18). "That ye put on the new man which, after God, is created in righteousness and true holiness" (Eph. 4:24).

4. It was Christ's mission to give us in this life complete deliverance from the nature as well as from the guilt of sin. "Who gave himself for us, that he might redeem us from all iniquity, and purify unto himself a peculiar people, zealous of good works" (Titus 2: 14). "Thou shalt call his name JESUS; for he shall save his people from their sins" (Matt. 1:21). "For this purpose the Son of God was manifested, that he might destroy the works of the devil" (1 John 3:8). "Ye know that he was manifested to take away our sins" (1 John 3:5).

5. We are commanded to be holy. "I am the Lord your God: ye shall therefore sanctify yourselves, and ye shall be holy; for I am holy" (Lev. 11:44). "Because it is written, Be ye holy; for I am holy" (1 Peter 1:16).

6. It is taught as an attained experience. "What shall we say then? Shall we continue in sin that grace may abound? God forbid. How shall we that are dead to sin live any longer therein" (Rom. 6: 1, 2)? "Knowing this, that our old man is crucified with him, that the body of sin might be destroyed, that henceforth we should not serve sin" (Rom. 6:6). "But now, being made free from sin, and become servants to God, ye have your fruit unto holiness, and the end everlasting life" (Rom. 6:22). "That we, being delivered out of the hand of our enemies, might serve him without fear, in

holiness and righteousness before him, all the days of our life" (Luke 1:74, 75).

It may be asked, "Can any examples of entire sanctification be found? Are there any who have lived this experience?" If one authentic case is produced, it puts those who deny the possibility of the experience where they must prove that there can be no others. There are many such examples mentioned in the word of God. "Noah was a just man and perfect in his generations, and Noah walked with God" (Gen. 6:9). "There was a man in the land of Uz, whose name was Job; and that man was perfect and up-right" (Job 1:1). "And they were both righteous before God, walking in all the commandments and ordinances of the Lord blameless" (Luke 1:6). "Ye are witnesses, and God also, how holily and justly and unblamably we behaved ourselves among you that believe" (1 Thes. 2:10).

Thousands of most credible witnesses have died with the profession that Christ had given them the experience of holiness, and that for years they had lived in peace, patience, and purity both of heart and life. Thousands more are living to-day in all denominations who constantly profess that Christ has given them an experience of perfect love. Shall we believe their testimony? Why not? God is no respecter of persons.

REV. WALTER A. SELLEW, A. M.,
Corresponding Editor of the Free Methodist

6
HOLINESS A PRIVILEGE

MR. WORCESTER'S DEFINITION of the word holy is, "(1) Pure in heart; free from sin; immaculate; good; pious; religious; devout." 'An *holy* angel' (2) Consecrated; hallowed; sacred; divine. 'In the *holy* Scriptures.'" His definition of the word holiness is, "(1) The state or quality of being holy, or free from sin; purity of heart; sanctity; piety.— Continue in faith and *holiness* (2) The state of being hallowed or consecrated; sacredness; divineness." You may notice that about the only difference in the terms "holy" and "holiness" is that the latter term refers to a fixed condition or state expressed by the former. The ending "ness" almost invariably indicates a fixed condition or state— as sinfulness; righteousness; wickedness, etc.

"Robinson's Calmet," or Bible Dictionary speaks thus on holiness: "Holy, Holiness. These terms sometimes denote outward purity or cleanliness; sometimes internal holiness. God is holy in a transcendent and infinitely perfect manner. He is the fountain of holiness, purity and innocency. He sanctifies his people and requires perfect holiness in those who approach him." The Lord, by the mouth of his servant Peter in the first chapter of his first epistle and sixteenth verse issues a plain, unmistakable command: "Be ye holy for I am holy." Here we are commanded to be or to become holy as he is or to become possessed of the kind— not degree— of holiness of which he is inherently possessed.

Let us notice in what this holiness consists. First I would say, negatively: purity; freedom from sin. "Thou art of purer eyes than to behold evil" (Hab. 1:13). "For there is no iniquity with the Lord our God" (2 Chron. 19:7). Positively: the fulness of love, filled with love; yea, love itself. "God is love." Now as we are commanded to "be holy" as he is, we will admit without argument that we must be possessed of the same kind— so must first be made free from sin, or sinfulness; and then be filled with love, yea, with perfect love. Has the Lord made provision in the economy of salvation for bringing about a so-much-desired result? I think so. Of the Savior it is written, "Who gave himself for us, that he might redeem us from all iniquity, and purify unto himself a peculiar people, zealous of good works" (Titus 2: 14). The apostle under divine inspiration prayed that the Ephesian church "might be filled with all the fulness of God"; and as "God is love" his fulness must be love; hence he prayed that they might be filled with love. First or negatively, men are redeemed from all iniquity (and iniquity is defined as "a wicked act, wickedness"); then "purified"— made clean— and then filled with holy love, thus coming into possession of holiness (in kind) like that which the Lord possesses. So when I speak of holiness as a privilege, I speak of this kind.

We understand by privilege "A peculiar benefit, advantage or favor; a right or immunity not enjoyed by others, or by all." —*Webster*. According to the word of God the privilege or right to become holy and enjoy all that comes or may come as a result of being holy belongs to all men. The provisions of the gospel are for all. "The grace of God that bringeth salvation hath appeared unto *all* men." —Titus. The gracious gospel invitations are to all. "Ho *every one* that thirsteth, come ye" —Isaiah. "Come unto me *all* ye that labor and are heavy laden and I will give you rest." —*Christ*. So this heavenly benefit, this wondrous right, this gracious advantage or favor is for all. Your God-given privilege is to be holy, as was Enoch. Your heaven-born right is to be righteous, as was Zacharias. It is yours, reader, to walk in the foot-steps of the holiest of men.

We must be careful to bear in mind that these wondrous privileges are conditioned privileges. "If we confess our sins, he is faithful and just to forgive us our sins." "If we walk in the light as he is in the light, we have fellowship one with another; and the blood of Jesus Christ his Son cleanseth us from all sin." That little conjunction "if" always indicates condition. Those who meet the conditions may enjoy the privileges.

A privilege affording us bodily comfort and satisfaction is appreciated and enjoyed, though it be but to take shelter in the stranger's barn and be thus far protected from the storm. To be invited to share his cozy sitting room and to occupy his comfortable couch is a greater privilege still. The privilege increases as we discover in the supposed stranger an old-time friend with whom we can enjoy congenial, instructive and elevating conversation, and who will allow us to revel in his vast library and hold audience with the greatest minds of earth. The privilege increases in value as we ascend from the gratifying of bodily to mental wants and desires. These privileges thus alluded to are temporal and necessarily limited and brief. But think of holiness as a privilege! This relates to my body, mind and spirit, throughout time and eternity. It is pardon now and pardon forever; peace now and forever; joy now and forever; soul rest now and forever; purity now and evermore; fellowship here and hereafter; oneness with all that is pure and good and grand and glorious, eternally.

"He that overcometh will I give to eat of the tree of life, which is in the midst of the paradise of God." God's holy heaven and all it contains is for the holy, and only for the holy.

Note in conclusion the following passages indicating your privileges: "Having therefore these promises, dearly beloved, let us cleanse ourselves from all filthiness of the flesh and spirit, perfecting holiness in the fear of God" (2 Cor. 7:1). "Having therefore, brethren, boldness to enter into the holiest by the blood of Jesus, by a new and living way, which he hath consecrated for us, through the vail, that is to say, his flesh; and having a high priest over the house of God; let us draw near with a true heart in full assurance of faith, having our hearts sprinkled from an evil conscience, and our bodies washed with pure water" (Heb. 10: 19-22). "Therefore leaving the principles of the doctrine of Christ, let us go on unto perfection… And this will we do, if God permit" (Heb. 6:1-3).

Rev. Charles B. Ebey,
Corresponding Editor of the Free Methodist

Rev. Burton Rensselaer Jones

7
HOLINESS A NECESSITY

THE TERM HOLINESS SUGGESTS the idea of wholeness, completeness. It is very comprehensive and includes "all things involved in complete salvation from sin" and the possession of the divine nature. Holiness is absolute moral purity and comprises the entire sanctification of the will, the affections and sensibilities. In its experience the secret, subtle life of self is destroyed and nothing contrary to pure love remains in the heart. Every faculty of the soul and every sense and power of the body is brought into harmonious action with the will of God.

In urging the necessity of holiness as a distinct work we are in accord with the teachings of John Wesley and leading Methodist writers. "The church is never in her true normal state except when she is holy. Holiness is her only divinely appointed ornament. Science and wealth have often ruined the church; her ornament and power are only in her purity." —*Holiness Manual.* "The doctrine of entire sanctification, as a distinct work wrought in the soul by the Holy Ghost, is the great distinguishing doctrine of Methodism. This given up and

we have little left which we do not hold in common with other evangelical denominations." —*Dr. Jesse T. Peck.*
That holiness is a necessity to the church of Christ is evident from the following considerations.
1. God wills that his people should be holy. This is clearly expressed in the scriptures. "For this is the will of God even your sanctification" (1 Thes. 4:3). What God wills that his children should attain must be regarded as of the greatest importance. Believers are to be cleansed from "all filthiness of the flesh and spirit" that they may be able to "perfect holiness in the fear of God." Licentiousness, depraved appetites, sensual indulgences— as they relate to the flesh— together with ill tempers, pride, worldly ambition, covetousness, harshness, revenge, deceit, self-seeking, and such like— as they relate to the spirit— are offensive to God and should be cleansed away. A leper once came to Jesus and "worshiped him, saying, Lord, if thou wilt, thou canst make me clean." It was the will of the leper to be cleansed, and he had faith that if the Master willed it the work would be done. "And Jesus put forth his hand and touched him, saying, I will; be thou clean. And immediately his leprosy was cleansed" (Matt. 8:2, 3). God wills the entire sanctification of every believer, and as soon as the believer makes that will his choice, no other power can prevent the work being done. It may be done immediately. In *Holiness Manual* we read, "This is God's will now, that we be sanctified. The will of God authorizes our sanctification; and when we put ourselves in perfect line with that will it will most surely be executed within us." In *Purity and Maturity* the author says, "Our purification is God's will in both the permissive and authoritative sense,... Duty and privilege are bound together in religious things; duty is privilege, and privilege is duty." All privileged attainments in the will of God are necessary to spiritual growth and development.

2. Holiness is included in the divine promises. And what God promises the soul needs. Purity was included in the old covenant. "And the Lord thy God will circumcise thine heart, and the heart of thy seed, to love the Lord thy God with all thine heart, and with all thy soul, that thou mayest live" (Deut. 30:6). According to the best authorities "the circumcision of the heart implies the purification of the soul from all unrighteousness." "Then will I sprinkle clean water upon you, and ye shall be clean: from all your filthiness, and from all your idols, will I cleanse you" (Ezek. 36:25).

The Gospel abounds in assurances of God's willingness, ability and faithfulness to sanctify his church. At the close of St. Paul's earnest prayer for the entire sanctification of the church at Thessalonica he adds, "Faithful is he that calleth you, who also will do it" (1 Thes. 5:23, 24). In 1 Jno. 1:9 it is written, "If we confess our sins, he is faithful and just to forgive us our sins, and to cleanse us from all unrighteousness." Here is an assurance of God's faithfulness to fulfil his promise, and that the promise comprehends the work of cleansing from all unrighteousness. These exceeding great and precious promises make it possible for believers to become "partakers of the divine nature." And the soul's necessities require that we measure up fully to this standard.

3. Its necessity is seen in the provision made. The infinite sacrifice made for the complete redemption of mankind from sin argues that nothing short of that will meet the divine requirement. In referring to the dawn of the gospel day the prophet says, "In that day there shall be a fountain opened to the house of David and to the inhabitants of Jerusalem for sin and uncleanness" (Zech. 13:1). Reference is here made to atonement provision for the cleansing of the human heart. The name given to the Son of Mary indicated his mission into the world: "Thou shalt call his name Jesus: for he shall save his people from their sins." Here is

provision for complete salvation from sin. Jesus came to "destroy the works of the devil." All sin is of the devil. Hence "the blood of Jesus Christ his Son cleanseth us from *all* sin." Thank God! Here is complete cleansing for every longing, believing soul.

4. God requires his people to be "clean" and "holy". Things non-essential are not required in the scriptures. Hence whatever God commands must be a necessity. That which God expresses as his will, includes in his promises and for which he has made provision in Christ he requires his children to attain. We cannot be guiltless and neglect to enter upon our purchased inheritance.

The word of the Lord to Israel was, "Ye shall be holy: for I the Lord your God am holy" (Lev. 19:2). These words are quoted by St. Peter as applicable to the church under the gospel dispensation. Jesus said to his disciples, "Be ye therefore perfect even as your Father which is in heaven is perfect." When asked what is the first commandment of the law the Savior replied, "Thou shalt love the Lord thy God with all thy heart, and with all thy soul, and with all thy mind." These words are imperative and clearly express the duty of every believer to seek the perfection of divine love in the heart. Yea, "The end of the commandment is charity [love] out of a pure heart, and of a good conscience, and of faith unfeigned." God does not require impossibilities, and this blessed experience may be attained through the provision he has made.

5. Holiness is necessary as a qualification for Christian duty. Life is attended with grave responsibilities. Mankind are not placed here simply to prepare for the hereafter. Personal happiness is not the Christian's highest aim. God is to be glorified and his will wrought out. Certain graces are to be exercised in this life which cannot be exercised in the life to come. To this end holiness is a necessity. (1) In a life of holiness we can prove our courage, fidelity and loyalty to God in the midst of persecution and opposition.

Along the line between sin and holiness the seat of war is located. There the enemy concentrates his forces, and there our graces are tested. There will be no enemies in heaven, and he who would prove himself a good soldier of Jesus Christ must do so in this world. Be brave here, stand by the right and prove your loyalty to truth and holiness in this land of enemies. When you reach the celestial city the last enemy will have been conquered— the last foe vanquished. (2) Here we can practice resignation to the divine will in the midst of sorrow and bereavement. To be able to say from the heart at all times, "Thy will be done in earth [in me] as it is in heaven," all inward corruption, all antagonistic desires and tendencies must be removed and the heart's submission, trust and love must be perfect Heart purity admits of no murmuring nor complaining against God amid the most afflicting providences. This grace cannot be exercised in heaven for "There'll be no sorrow there." (3) The grace of pure, disinterested benevolence is to be exercised in a life of holiness. To feed the hungry, clothe the naked, visit the sick, build churches, endow schools, and otherwise support the cause of God, as opportunity offers and means warrant, is the work of practical holiness. Some Christians are intending to be exceedingly generous after they die, but their generosity often falls into the lap of the unscrupulous lawyer or of undeserving heirs. True holiness is needed to open the fountain of beneficence in this life. Such acts of kindness and deeds of charity cannot be performed in heaven. No suffering enters there. "In heaven are found no sons of want."

6. Holiness is necessary to the highest degree of usefulness. At conversion even the disciples of Christ were not fully qualified for their important calling. Jesus said to them, "Tarry ye at the city of Jerusalem until ye be endued with power from on high", assuring them that they should receive power after the Holy Ghost had come upon them. They needed the pentecostal baptism to prepare them for

their life-work. When with one accord assembled the mighty baptism of refining fire came upon the church. As a result a sweeping revival broke out and thousands were converted to God and added to the church. Pentecostal power is necessary to insure revivals of the pentecostal type. There is real eloquence in a holy life. It speaks in certain tones to all with whom its possessor associates, and reaches hearts that no arguments can reach and no reasoning convince. Mr. Wesley instructed his ministers to "urge the converts on to holiness", for in this lay the secret of their stability and their power for usefulness.

7. Holiness is necessary for admission to heaven. "Follow peace with all men, and holiness without which no man shall see the Lord" (Heb. 12:14). No matter what else one may possess, without holiness he is not qualified for heaven. Only the "pure in heart" shall see God. He who entertains the hope of seeing Christ as he is must "purify himself even as he [Christ] is pure." Fair professions, splendid gifts, extensive learning, without holiness will not answer the divine claim. They are like the corpse that has the human form but lacks the life — the soul.

Rev. Burton Rensselaer Jones,
General Superintendent of the Free Methodist Church

8
HOLINESS AS RELATED TO JUSTIFICATION AND SANCTIFICATION

JUSTIFICATION IS AN ACT or sentence of God whereby a sinner, recognized as guilty, upon the exercise of penitent faith in Christ as a substitute who has borne his sins, is pardoned and accepted into divine favor. At the same moment God does this he imparts the Holy Spirit who regenerates (implants divine life by which the soul is "born of God"), adopts and witnesses to the penitent that he is made a child of God. So Dr. Pope and Richard Watson agree. Wesley seems to make the regeneration consequent on the Spirit's testimony of adoption. A justified state is inclusive of all these experiences. The power of sin inward and outward— of indwelling sin, observe— is broken. The love of God is shed abroad in the heart of such, and the obligation is then pressed upon them (Rom. 6:19), "As ye have yielded your members servants to uncleanness and to iniquity unto iniquity, so now present your members servants of righteousness unto holiness." "*Righteousness* here is a conformity to the divine will; *holiness*, to the whole divine nature" *(Wesley's Notes).*

Hearty submission to the divine will is a characteristic of a state of justification. It leads to holiness. But there is a material difference. Indwelling sin, while defiling and enslaving the entire man, body, mind and will, has its chief seat in the involuntary powers of the soul—the affections and desires. The awakened sinner says, "To will is present with me, but how to perform what is good I find not." As he deepens in penitence and conviction, he says, "I delight in the law of God after the inward man." Still he is enslaved by "another law in his members". These "members" are "the desires of the flesh [body] and of the mind" (Eph. 2:3; Col. 3:5), called in Gal. 5:24 "the flesh, with the affections and lusts". The regenerate (justified) man is enabled to present his members unto God as instruments of righteousness. He yet finds, however, much resistance in them, and all his moral powers and exercises contaminated and weakened by the presence of the sin that still dwelleth in him.

Sanctification, though closely allied to holiness, is rather a process of making holy than holiness itself. In its more common use it recognizes the presence of sin, and makes holy by a process or act of purification. Holiness does not necessarily regard sin, only as its eternal opposite and antagonist when contemplated. God, angels, Christ, are holy without sanctification in this sense. Their holiness is a positive quantity—a fulness of rectitude, a quality of character and disposition positively loving and promoting truth and righteousness. Our holiness is God-likeness—godliness—also a positive quantity. It is effected, however, by purification.

Sanctification, then, answers to all those expressions, acts, or processes, by which "the old man" is put off, "the flesh" or "carnal mind" purged out, "the body of sin" destroyed. Hence the propriety of considering it both as a process and an act— rather a process admitting of definite, instantaneous completion— as in Wesley's illustration of a man gradually dying and at length expiring. There is nothing in the nature of the case limiting its meaning to either a process or an act alone. Whatever removes carnality from the thoughts, affections, imaginations, desires, purposes, words or actions of a man, either positively or negatively manifested, does by so much sanctify him and increase his holiness. But the purport of the crucifixion of "our old man" is "that the body of sin might be destroyed" — as truly so as that a man nailed to a cross should shortly expire. Completed sanctification results in perfected holiness.

We should note that the divine life implanted in conversion, with all its expressions of thought, affections, purposes and aspirations, is holy. And inasmuch as this new life is made predominant in the soul when implanted, so as to control and describe the character of the man, he is thus made truly (though not fully) holy in a state of justification. The graces of this Spirit-begotten life are capable of growth, and growth in holiness is promoted by sanctification. Unlimited, unhindered growth requires the complete extirpation of opposite tempers and desires, by entire sanctification.

1. Justification as an act reconciles a man to God and is prerequisite to all holiness.

2. As a state it includes true holiness in its beginnings and constitutes a holy man. This should be clearly apprehended and upheld; otherwise we shall have spurious conversions, false professions, inconsistent living and a worldly church. Yet it should not be used to grieve the children of God, whose adoption is scripturally recognized in spite of many defects and inconsistencies.

3. Sanctification is both a process and an act of purification of heart and life from remaining sin. Chiefly it concerns the destruction of indwelling sin as a defiling prin-

ciple diffused throughout the soul. If we are too stringent in its limitation we shall fail of thoroughness in our investigation and confession of sin in its manifold existence and workings. If we are too diffuse in our dealing we shall lop off the branches and leave the root of the tree in the heart.

4. Holiness is conformity to and agreement with God in his thoughts, feelings, disposition and attitude toward truth and righteousness, toward sin and sinners. Sanctification is the means of perfecting it in quality, and endless growth of increasing it in degree.

5. Entire holiness is infinitely obligatory and important.

REV. CHARLES M. DAMON,
Ex-President of Orleans College

9
CONVICTION FOR HOLINESS

THE POWER OF SEEING is possible only in the presence of light. When God gives spiritual light, he gives knowledge of spiritual things and conditions. "The entrance of thy words giveth light." God's word is a revelation of spiritual truth which gives us the knowledge of God himself.

The sinner is under a total eclipse of this knowledge until awakened. In conviction the gloom begins to be mingled with foregleams of the coming day. The rising Sun of righteousness begins to dispel the night before he appears on the horizon. As time progresses "the bright and morning Star" appears in token of coming day. Faith and hope begin to dawn, though dimly, within the awakened mind. As light increases he begins to observe that he is clad in tatters, and a little later that these are covered with filth, while his substance is all spent, and he is left a pauper and an alien from the commonwealth of Israel. He is worse than that, but in the midst of these distracting external revelations do not add to his misery the disclosure of internal corruption. He has enough now to sink a soul in eternal despair, but for the sight of the morning Star, which betokens the dawning of a better day.

Still the light increases, and at length the day is born. "The day star hath arisen in his heart" to give "the light of the knowledge of the glory of God in the face of Jesus Christ." Now he can sing,

> "Long my imprisoned spirit lay,
>   Fast bound in sin and nature's night;
> Thine eye diffused a quickening ray,
>   I rose,— the dungeon flamed with light."

As time progresses new and more appalling discoveries of inbred sin are made, and all hope and faith would collapse if the vision continued; but in mercy God tempers the revelation. (Do not despise the "dark hours" in the justified relation— they are seasons of special mercy.) A uniform testimony runs through orthodox churches to this unhappy discovery following every genuine conversion. And this discovery and conviction must necessarily precede and form a part of a conviction for holiness. By the light which enters the heart at conversion the discovery of the corrupt internal condition is made. In the absence of this light inbred sin may be honestly denied as existing, but seldom by one a fortnight after a true conversion. When the discovery is made, the question is pressed immediately, what shall be done? The preachers have many theories. But the soul ready to cut off right hands or pluck out right eyes in order to gain a right knowledge of God's will, turns to the Bible to see what God says he should do about it. He therein learns the name of what he has discovered. It is called "the body of sin," the carnal mind," the "old man." Next in his search he discovers what to do with it— "Our old man is crucified... that the body of sin might be destroyed." Knowing that crucifixion is accomplished only this side the grave he begins to search for the time when the matter may be accomplished; and learns that even now all inward sin may be put away, for "If we walk in the light as he is in the light... the blood of Jesus Christ... cleanseth us from *all* sin." He also discovers his part in the operation to be one of confession and renunciation.

Conviction for holiness comes as any other conviction comes— by light. Standing in the broad light of day a man with eyes can no more honestly doubt or deny his surroundings and the matters of fact concerning them than he can deny his own existence. The light is reflected by sanctified lives. Hence the need of setting "living epistles" of holiness before the church and the world, who may be "read and known of all men." "Let your light [of holiness] so shine before men, that they may see your good works, and glorify your Father which is in heaven." Perhaps we complain that the doctrine of holiness is not received as extensively and as fully as it should be, but are we setting an undeniable example of holy living before men? The preacher has not delivered his soul when he has preached the doctrine; he is just as fully obligated to set before his flock and the world a holy life as a holy doctrine. Character cannot be hid from public view— it will out. God will not let it be hid, whatever its quality. Influence is the radiating heat and light of internal character. Let us not wonder, then, at so little or so feeble conviction for holiness, while we fail to set before the gaze of men an example which is "a burning and a shining light," and whose diffusing rays so light up the moral darkness of the world that men will know that we have been with Jesus and learned of him. He has said, "And I, if I be lifted up from the earth, will draw all men unto me." Lift him up on the cross— allow men to gaze upon you in a thousand tribulations, on a thousand crosses, manifesting and revealing the spirit and patience of Jesus Christ— and our altars will be filled, as of yore, with seekers of Bible holiness.

Rev. A.J. M'Kinney,
Of the Colorado Conference

[As pertinent to the subject discussed in the foregoing paper, and because of its adaptation to throw light on another phase of the subject, we here subjoin the following anonymous item. —EDITOR.]

The conviction for holiness or entire sanctification which a believer experiences, and by which he is led to seek for full and perfect conformity to the divine likeness, is not a conviction of guilt or condemnation upon his soul, as too many have supposed. The fact is, entire freedom from condemnation is the only condition in which it is possible successfully to seek for inward and complete sanctification. Nor is conviction for holiness a conviction of backslidings, all of which need to be repented and forgiven the same as other sins. A felt need of more religion is not conviction for holiness; since there is no state of grace in which this may not be experienced, and in a justified state it may be experienced without any clear apprehension of what inbred sin is, or of the necessity of being cleansed therefrom. A conscious lack of power for service, though it may enter into or accompany conviction for holiness, does not of itself constitute the conviction of which we speak.

What then does constitute true and proper conviction for holiness? We answer: It is a persuasion wrought by the Holy Spirit in the heart of the justified believer, (1) Of a lack of inward conformity to all the will of God; (2) Of the existence of positively depraved or sinful propensities and tendencies within him, which struggle for ascendency [sic] and are only subdued by grace; (3) Of the provision made by the will of God, through the atonement and by the gift of the Holy Spirit, for the removal of all inward sin, and the investiture of the soul with all spiritual virtues unmixed with moral evil; (4) Of the necessity of immediate and perfect inward cleansing; all of which is accompanied with a loathing of carnal self, and a restless, yearning desire to be pure in heart and filled with all the fulness of God. He who experiences such a conviction is surely not far from the kingdom of "perfect love."

We must express it, however, as our firm belief that the way in which many preach and teach holiness at the present time misleads scores of supposed seekers of this grace, inducing them to rest in a superficial experience for a time, from which, at length, they turn to a more worldly and carnal life than they indulged before. It is assumed by not a few of these teachers that all professors of religion, no matter how backslidden they may have been in heart or how inconsistent and crooked in life, are in a state at once to believe for and receive the sanctifying grace of God; whereas multitudes of them have need of repentance, confession, restitution and pardon before they can be in a justified state and able properly to apprehend their need of sanctifying grace or to exercise requisite faith for its reception. One of the greatest needs of the "holiness movement" of to-day is such a type of preaching and teaching as will produce a deeper conviction of inbred sin, and a correspondingly higher conception of the nature and fruit of true holiness.

10
CONSECRATION AND HOLINESS

1. HOLINESS. BY HOLINESS I MEAN 1. The completion of the work of saving grace in the heart of a justified believer, cleansing it from all sin, thus making it perfectly pure in God's sight: no wrong temper, nothing contrary to love remaining in the heart.
  2. The heart thus made pure, filled with love to God and man, so that the believer loves God with all his heart, and his neighbor as himself, in accordance with the divine command.
  3. Subsequent walking before the Lord in all the commandments of the Lord blameless, doing the will of God from the heart.
  This kind of holiness, which is called "true holiness," I believe to be in substance what many writers mean by such phrases as, "Entire sanctification," "Perfect Love," "The Higher Life," etc. It begins the moment one is truly converted to God, or, in other words, is "justified by faith"; but it is not finished then, but may be finished subsequently as far as cleansing the heart from sin and filling it with love is concerned, *instantaneously*, whenever the believer

fully trusts in the atoning blood of Christ for it. "The very God of peace sanctify you wholly; and I pray God your whole spirit, soul and body be preserved blameless unto the coming of our Lord Jesus Christ. Faithful is he that calleth you, who also will do it" (1 Thes. 5:23-24). "In whom also after that ye believed, ye were sealed with that holy Spirit of promise" (Eph. 1:13).

II. *Consecration.* By consecration I mean that solemn, sacred and *entire dedication* of one's self to the service of God, which is made subsequent to conversion and prior to the complete purification of the heart. This none can truly make unless deeply moved and led thereto by the Holy Spirit of God. That there is such a work of special and entire consecration, which is the act of the creature, by divine assistance, appears to be both rational and scriptural; and, if so, essential — as far as light is given — to the completion of the work of saving grace here, and the subsequent abiding of the soul in entire holiness before God.

As a rule, the awakened, penitent seeker after pardon and divine acceptance has but little understanding of God's requirements other than that he must abandon his sins, submit himself to God and accept of Christ. This submission or surrender of the sinner to God is probably regarded by some theorists as entire consecration. The most, I think, that can properly be said of it is, it is a *wholesale* consecration. That the seeker after pardon, whose mind is darkened concerning spiritual things, and who is exercised with a depressing sense of guilt and condemnation, should have a clear sense of what entire consecration to the service of God means, is scarcely supposable.

But subsequent to "being justified by faith," and while walking "in the light as God is in the light," the believer in due time comes to the place in his experience where he feels, not a sense of loss, but of the need of a *pure heart*, of a more perfect conformity to all the divine will, — a longing of soul after all the fulness of God. And it is here, just at this point of experience, that in the effort to obtain this second state of grace, the Holy Spirit's light shines clearer than ever before on the Christian pathway, and now the Holy Spirit begins to itemize to the believer what was included in the divine purpose by the required unconditional surrender when pardon was sought and found.

Following this itemizing operation of the Holy Spirit is the believer's *entire consecration*, in which he must evermore sacredly hold himself before the Lord. His intellect, with all its faculties; his soul, with all its propensities and powers; his heart, with all its capacity to love the good and hate the evil; his reputation, to be divinely cared for while he obeys his Master; his body — its eyes, ears, tongue, hands, feet, all — for no profane use, but for use in harmony with the will of God; all worldly possessions laid at the Redeemer's feet to be henceforth righteously used, — all, ALL, *now and forever the Lord's!*

With such a devotement of one's self to the Lord, and which to many means vastly more in the itemizing operation of the Holy Spirit than I can here narrate, the soul may launch out on the sanctifying promises of God, go down under the cleansing blood of Christ, and arise entirely renewed in the life and love of God. Amen!

"I beseech you therefore brethren, by the mercies of God, that ye present your bodies a living sacrifice, holy, acceptable unto God, which is your reasonable service; and be not conformed to this world: but be ye transformed by the renewing of your minds, that ye may prove what is that good, and acceptable, and perfect will of God" (Rom. 12:1-2). This message was "To all that be in Rome, beloved of God, called to be saints," which means holy ones. All God's people are called to be holy ones, completely holy. Hence they should heed the exhortation given to the Romans, and present their bodies (a part is here put for the whole) "a living sacrifice, holy, acceptable unto God," that so all forbidden worldly conformity may cease, and there may be a complete transformation by the renewing of the mind. Thus may they "prove what is that good, and acceptable, and perfect will of God," — which is the sanctification of "the whole spirit, soul and body."

Rev. Moses N. Downing,
Corresponding Editor of the Free Methodist

11
THE REVELATION OF FAITH TO HOLINESS

IN THE PROCESS OF SALVATION there are successive steps, by which the soul is led out of darkness into light. But the final step which brings one into the kingdom of God's dear Son is faith in the Lord Jesus Christ. There are some things, however, which naturally precede faith as necessary conditions of the same, and which should be well considered.

First, *the understanding must be divinely enlightened.* There must be, to some degree, a revelation of the divine character before it is possible for man to "believe that God is, and that he is a rewarder of them that diligently seek him." The Spirit must "convince of sin, of righteousness and of judgment," thus making man feel the necessity of a Saviour, before he can be led to believe the things necessary to salvation. How can a soul dead in sin be conscious of its condition until awakened by the Spirit of the living God? "How shall they believe in him of whom they have not heard? And how shall they hear without a preacher?" (Rom. 10:14.) The eyes of our understanding must be opened to behold our spiritual necessities before we can reasonably be expected to exercise that faith in God which alone can render us acceptable to him; and by means divinely appointed God provides for the enlightenment of all men.

Another process which necessarily precedes the exercise of saving faith is *entire consecration of self and all its interests to God*. This is our part in the great work of salvation. It must proceed from a firm conviction that God is infinite both in wisdom and goodness— that he knows what is for our highest good and from his very nature is morally bound to require of us only that which is essential to the same. Convinced of this, there must be an entire surrender of the human to the divine will before we can with confidence seek additional light or blessing.

Again, we must by a rigid denial of carnal self and a perfect resignation to the divine will *exercise ourselves unto godliness* if we would attain unto saving faith. Thus we must "strive to enter in at the strait gate." To strive, according to the scriptural sense, is to agonize. This is the original word. Not that we must wait for an agony of feeling before we begin this important work— this is not the scriptural idea. Striving is an allusion to the Grecian contests in which the competitors were expected to exert themselves to the utmost to win the crown which was to be placed upon the victors brow. Thus the contestants were said to strive (agonize) in the race for victory. So, by rigid self-denial, thorough consecration to God and continual waiting upon him in the appointed means of grace, viz., watching, fasting, Bible reading, meditation and prayer, must we exercise ourselves unto godliness, if we would attain unto that faith without which it is impossible to please him.

But we must beware of trusting or resting in this "exercise" on our part as anything meritorious in the sight of God. This would be seeking salvation by works; whereas it is written, "By grace are ye saved *through faith*" These are not works of righteousness or merit, but "fruits meet for repentance", and such as bring the soul into that changed attitude before God, where it can confidently look to him to be supplied "with all spiritual blessings" in Christ. Nor does feeling necessarily have anything to do with this except to follow as a result. God enlightens our understanding concerning his own character and requirements, and as to our necessities and duties. This may be but is not necessarily accompanied by any great degree of emotion. In that light we abase and deny self and surrender our all to the divine will until we are conscious that in this respect we have made a complete offering before the Lord. Then have we reached the point where we can and may exercise that faith which is the final and absolute condition of salvation from sin.

"But what", says one, "is the faith which sanctifies? What am I to believe in order to salvation?" And someone replies, "Why, just believe you are saved, that is all." And the mind of that inquirer naturally replies, within itself at least, "But I know I am not saved, and will believing a falsity make it a fact?" And here many get into perplexity which often leads them either to despair or else to rest in a superficial show of godliness, either of which extreme is dangerous and often fatal. What then are we to believe as the final condition of deliverance from sin?

First, we must *believe in ourselves* — that we have fully met, on our part, all the conditions previous and necessary to a simple faith, according to the revealed will of God. When our offering has been made perfect before the Lord, his promises are, "I will receive you." I will sprinkle clean water upon you and ye shall be clean; from all your filthiness and from all your idols will I cleanse you;" and, "the blood of Jesus Christ his Son cleanseth us from all sin." These are promises which God has declared shall be fulfilled when we thus seek him with undivided hearts.

The second thing we are to believe is that the word of God in these promises of deliverance from sin through the blood of his Son Jesus Christ is now fulfilled in us.

Mr. Wesley's way of explaining the faith by which we are sanctified was this: It is a divine evidence or condition (1) That God hath promised it [sanctification] in the holy Scriptures; (2) That what God hath promised he is able to perform; (3) That he is able and willing to do it now; (4) That *he now doeth it* (Sermons, Vol. I. pp. 390, 391). Believing this, we should rest in that belief. "And he that believeth [this] hath the witness in himself" — his own consciousness bearing witness to the fact. When our faith is thus made perfect, God seals the finished work of grace by the gift of the Holy Ghost. Then, in addition to the witness of our own consciousness, "The Spirit himself beareth witness with our spirit" that we are purified from sin.

But the victory over sin achieved by this instantaneous exercise of faith is not a sufficient guarantee of future exemption from sin. It is "by faith we have access into this grace", and it is plainly written, "by faith ye stand." The exercise of faith by which we overcame sin yesterday will not secure us against temptation to-day. The food that nourished us yesterday does not meet the physical demands of to-day. Faith sustains the same relation to a life of holiness that the process of respiration does to physical life. To cease from breathing is to die. To cease from the constant exercise of faith is to lose the life of God from the soul. Hence it is written, "The just shall live by faith."

Faith, then, is *the fundamental and essential element of all holiness* in the creatures of God's moral government. "And without faith it is impossible to please him." Therefore in providing for the restoration of fallen humanity to its forfeited estate, God saw that the only plan of salvation by which man could be reharmonized with the principles of divine government was that of salvation by faith. Accordingly the whole plan of redemption is thus arranged. Hence it is written, "Now to him that worketh not, but believeth on him that justifieth the ungodly, his faith is counted to him for righteousness" (Rom. 4:5). The word of God likewise teaches that we are 'justified by faith," "sanctified by faith," "saved by faith," "kept by faith"; and that to gain eternal life we must "live by faith," "walk by faith," hold fast the profession of our faith, and finally that "This is the victory that overcometh the world, even our faith." Thus we see that faith is essential to holiness just as a foundation is essential to a perfect and permanent superstructure, or just as respiration is necessary to physical life. Hence a holy life is emphatically a life of faith. This accords with Paul's declaration: "The life that I now live, I live by the faith of the Son of God, who loved me and gave himself for me." Such is the relation of faith to holiness, considered either as a moral condition or as applied to moral action.

Since without faith it is impossible to please God, it follows that holiness can be retained only by a momentary or habitual exercise of faith. The instant we distrust God we displease him and bring darkness on our own hearts. Nor can any works which we may do be pleasing to him only as they spring from faith and are wrought with a single eye to glorify his name. The whole superstructure of Christian character, therefore, is built upon faith in God. "Having therefore, brethren, boldness [liberty] to enter into the holiest by the blood of Jesus, by a new and living way which he hath consecrated for us through the veil, that is to say, his flesh; and having a high priest over the house of God; let us draw near with a true heart, in full assurance of faith, having our hearts sprinkled from an evil conscience, and our bodies washed with pure water' (Heb. 10:19-22).

Rev. Wilson T. Hogg,
Editor of the Free Methodist

12
Fruits of Holiness

The word "fruit" is from the Latin verb *fruor* which means "to enjoy;" and hence, in its primary sense it has been defined as "Whatever is produced for the enjoyment of man or animals by the processes of vegetable growth." But the term is frequently used metaphorically especially in the Bible, in which sense it is defined as "The result, consequence, or effect of anything, whether beneficial or otherwise." Jesus attached a good deal of importance to the fruit of the life as an index of the character. When warning his disciples against false prophets he said, "Ye shall know them by their fruits." John the Baptist called for "fruits meet for repentance," while Paul desired the church to have "fruit unto holiness".

In a very important sense the fruit that springs from the heart and life of every Christian, regardless of the state of grace that may be enjoyed, is the spirit of holiness. The fruit of the Spirit is the fruit of holiness, and Paul says, "The fruit of the Spirit is love, joy, peace, long-suffering, gentleness, goodness, faith, meekness, temperance" (Gal.

5:22,23). But, while every Christian has the fruit of the Spirit, it remains for those who are wholly sanctified, and who are growing in grace, to "bring forth," "with patience, the peculiar fruit that God designs his children to produce. If the fruit is "unto holiness" there must exist a holy heart, and if fruit is brought forth to "perfection" it will take "patience". Fruit is also defined as "The ultimate product or result of a growth or development." The one who does not grow spiritually will be barren and unfruitful. The Christian graces enumerated by Peter (2 Peter 1:5-7) must be *abounding in us*, if we would be fruitful in the knowledge of our Lord Jesus Christ. But if this condition of soul exists— "if these things be in you and abound"— if we are "made free from sin," then the fruits of holiness will spring forth spontaneously. They will be natural and easy and there will be nothing hard or difficult about their production. "A good tree cannot bring forth evil fruit." It will not be difficult to show to the world that we love God with "all the heart" when his love has been "shed abroad" in the heart "by the Holy Ghost".

The fruit of holiness is of a superior quality. God's people do not produce poor, worm-eaten, sour fruit. There is nothing second-class about holiness, and its effects upon a community are always beneficent. The wisdom that cometh from above is "full of mercy and *good fruits*, without partiality and without hypocrisy" (Jas. 3: 17). Holiness is intensely practical. It works, it labors, it toils for others. It is self-forgetful, doing good and forgetting it and going on to accomplish greater good. It is "easy to be entreated" and is not stubborn or self-willed. In the inner life of the one entirely sanctified there will, under all circumstances, be proper emotions and feelings. In persecution and trial, as well as in the midst of sunshine and blessing, there will be an unruffled peace, a constant flow of joy, and a love for all mankind— even our enemies— which is unbroken. All the manifestations of the life will be in harmony with God and his truth. "The fruit of the Spirit is in all goodness, and righteousness and truth" (Eph. 5:9).

The fruit that springs from a holy heart will be in abundance and without cessation. Jesus said to his disciples, "Herein is my Father glorified that ye bear much fruit" (Jno. 15:8); and "the tree of life," which stood by the river that proceeded out of the throne of God (Rev. 22:1, 2), "yielded her fruit every month". In like manner it is the privilege of God's people not only to produce "much" fruit, but to have a constant yield "every month," all the year through. It is not enough occasionally to perform good deeds. God wants every action right and all the manifestations of the life in harmony with his will. Paul desired the Colossian brethren to be "fruitful in every good work," and to the Corinthians he used language quite similar, stating that God was able to make them "abound to every good work" (2 Cor. 9:8). It is the privilege of every one to have the "hundred fold" yield. "He that goeth forth and weepeth, bearing precious seed, shall doubtless come again with rejoicing, bringing his sheaves with him" (Psa. 126:6).

The fruit of holiness is of a lasting nature. It has in it the elements of hardiness and endurance. The disciples were to have fruit that should remain (Jno. 15:16). Hard winters and spring frosts will not injure it, and droughts or floods will have no effect upon it. Trials and afflictions only assist in maturing and enlarging the yield. Satan will use every effort to destroy all that is destructible, but a life bedded in holiness cannot be destroyed. The influence of such a life will never end, and the fruit produced will keep on multiplying as long as time shall last. We should consider well the great privilege we enjoy in being able to magnify Christ and garner sheaves for eternal life, thus erecting for ourselves a memorial far more lasting and precious than any granite of earth; for "They that be wise shall shine as the brightness of the firmament; and they that turn many to righteousness as the stars for ever and ever" (Dan. 12:3).

Let us remember that it is impossible not to bring forth fruit of some kind. To be spiritually barren is to be carnally fruitful, and the consequences of such a course will be most terrible. God has a right to expect and require a bounteous yield of good fruit from the life of every one; and it is sad indeed to think of appearing at the judgment with "nothing but leaves". God grant that all who read these lines may have their "fruit unto holiness, and the end everlasting life" (Rom. 6:22).

Rev. W.B. Olmstead,
Of the Ohio Conference

13
Professing Holiness

In considering the subject of holiness it is to be constantly remembered that entire sanctification is a part, the crowning part if you choose, of God's great work of salvation; but it is not a work of grace that can be separated from the work of salvation. Hence much that is said of the necessity of securing, retaining, or professing this manifestation of God's power to save, will apply with equal force to other stages of the work of salvation. Holiness is the logical and scriptural sequence of justification. If it is reasonable to believe that God would forgive and save a man from the guilt of sin, I hold it to be more reasonable to believe that he will save him from the power and dominion of inbred sin, which is the parent source of that guilt, to save humanity from which the Son of God himself must come to Calvary.

1. Professing holiness is *obligatory* on the part of all who experience it. The convert tells of his salvation, first, that the world of sinners may know that there is the power and willingness in God to pardon the guilt of past offenses, and that knowing this the unsaved may be led by an awak-

ened hope to repent of their sins and seek salvation. For the same reason one who is wholly sanctified should witness to the church and the world the willingness and power of God to save from the inbeing of sin, to cleanse the heart from all unrighteousness, so that those who are struggling with evil dispositions, with envyings, with anger and with the roots of bitterness may know there is power in Israel's God not only to give the victory over these evil dispositions, but so to fill their hearts with the presence of the Holy Spirit that their very being shall be so transformed that they will love as naturally, because of the heaven-born love reigning in them, as the child breathes. Thus by their testimony others will be led into a life of self-abandonment and trust in the divine grace into which they might not otherwise come from lack of light.

As it is the duty of witnesses to tell not only the truth but the whole truth, so he who holds back his word of testimony to the full power of God as he has experienced it becomes an unfaithful witness to the extent that he does hold back; and if we are not faithful to God how can we expect to continue in the divine favor to the extent of enjoying the cleansing power of the Holy Spirit? In fact a testimony to the power of God to cleanse from sin is necessary for the continued enjoyment of this power, inasmuch as it is both the witness and the expression of the soul's sincerity and fidelity to God.

The convert tells of salvation, second, that God may be glorified, as the changed manner of life is ascribed to the power of regenerating grace. So those who have been purified by the Holy Spirit and have been so transformed that perfect love reigns in their hearts owe it to God, as a matter of honesty, that they ascribe the dominion of heavenly tempers in them to his grace, lest others think that it proceeds from favoring circumstances, the absence of trials, the happiness of their surroundings, or from a naturally good disposition. We are told that our God is a jealous God, and when the Israelites were about to enter Canaan they were instructed in Deuteronomy twenty-sixth chapter, that after they had come into the land they should take of the first fruits of the earth in a basket and go unto the priest and make formal profession before him saying, "I profess this day unto the Lord thy God that I am come unto the country which the Lord sware unto our fathers for to give us." Every argument that can be advanced against the profession of holiness can, it seems to me, be refuted by a consideration of this commandment. Why should God want them to go before the priest and make a profession of a fact that was so clear to everyone? *They* knew they were in the land, for they had suffered much to get there. *God* knew it, for he had endured much in bringing them there: and their neighbors certainly knew it, for they had suffered much at their hands in coming there. So it was necessary neither for the information of their neighbors nor for the instruction of God, that they should make such a profession. Why then was it required? Because God chose this simple method of bringing them to witness to his great faithfulness and power. They were his witnesses, formal witnesses, that God had fulfilled his promises; and thus their own testimony would stand as a lasting rebuke to any thing like unbelief on their part. So again we see that the profession of holiness is desirable and necessary that the words of our own mouth may stand not only as a monument of God's grace, but as a barrier to the incoming of unbelief or doubt, in the moment of trial, as to the power and willingness of God to work out for us a great salvation.

 2. But if the fact of making a verbal profession of the power of God's grace in us is important, the *manner* in which such profession is made is no less important. The end of all such profession is, that God may be glorified in the salvation of others. This end must be held in view constantly, else the very end will be defeated. A flippant manner will bring conviction to none. Whatever serves to exalt self will

answer no good purpose. The confession of a naturally depraved nature and an acknowledgment of God's power to transform what was naturally repulsive may lead some to fresh hopes and courage. It will do more to aid souls into light than glib phrases such as we sometimes hear.

Said a godly man when he was asked why he did not more fully proclaim his enjoyment of this grace, "It is a great thing to be perfect in love, perfect in humility, perfect in submission." A deep sense of human unworthiness and God's condescension and marvellous power working in us will conduce to faithful testimony, purged of self-satisfaction. A conceited profession or professor makes more enemies than friends to the cause, and does more harm than good. Kept by divine grace in a spirit of humility we may speak without fear of the goodness, mercy and power of God.

BENSON HOWARD ROBERTS, A.M.,
Principal of A.M. Chesbrough Seminary

"Suppose one had attained to this, would you advise him to speak of it?

"At first perhaps he would scarce be able to refrain, the fire would be so hot within him; his desire to declare the loving-kindness of the Lord carrying him away like a torrent. But afterward he might; and then it would be advisable not to speak of it to them that know not God (it is most likely it would only provoke them to contradict and blaspheme); nor to others, without some particular reason, without some good end in view. Then he should have especial care *to avoid all appearance of boasting*; to speak with deepest humility and reverence, giving all the glory to God.
—*Wesley's Christian Perfection.*

14
RETAINING HOLINESS

> "And the Lord make you to increase and abound in love... to the end he may stablish your hearts unblameable in holiness before God, even our Father, at the coming of our Lord Jesus Christ with all his saints" (1 Thess. 3: 12, 13).

WE MUST GROW or die. This is a law of nature and grace. When the tree or plant ceases to grow it begins to decay. If we would keep from falling we must "grow in grace and in the knowledge of our Lord and Savior Jesus Christ." We shall get more or lose what we have. The law of the kingdom is to "lay up treasure in heaven," so to use our capital that it shall increase.

Turning to 2 Peter 1:4-11, we see that we may not only once have been enabled to grasp these exceeding great and precious promises, but, by adding virtue to virtue, grace to grace, thus making our calling and election sure, we may be *kept from falling*, and so gain an abundant entrance into the everlasting kingdom of our Lord. If we grow it will be because our spiritual nature has food adapted to it and in sufficient quantity. Certainly those who have attained to perfect love can no longer flourish on milk alone, but must have meat in order to grow strong. The truth as declared by God's servants, good reading of various kinds, but above all the study of God's word and waiting on God in prayer are means of growth. "Let the word of Christ dwell in you richly in all wisdom."

"If we walk in the light, as he is in the light, we have fellowship one with another, and the blood of Jesus Christ his Son cleanseth us from all sin" (1 Jno. 1:7). Both these verbs, "walk" and "cleanseth," are in the present tense. The important question is not whether once we had the experience of holiness, but does the blood of Jesus cleanse now? This is conditioned on walking in the light. The light grows brighter, day by day. The way of self-denial, sacrifice and service becomes clearer as we walk with God in purity of heart. We cannot go backward. It is always forward and upward. Gladly receiving light from any source God may be pleased to give, we must be committed to walk in it, depending on him for the needed grace. Every day, every hour, walking in the light of God we shall have the sweet fellowship promised, and shall find in our hearts the blessed witness that his blood cleanseth from all sin.

"If ye keep my commandments ye shall abide in my love" (Jno. 15:10), teaches in substance the same truth as above. For surely abiding in Jesus' love is "perfect love" and keeping God's commandments is identical with walking in the light. The Holy Ghost, through whose indwelling the heart is kept clean, is given "to them that obey him." There can be no sanctification, no progress in the spiritual life unless there be a constant yielding to God and a perfect acquiescence in all his known will.

Again, 1 Peter 1:5, teaches us that we are *"kept by the power of God."* While we must walk in the light and obey God's commandments we should never forget that we are utterly unable to keep ourselves. It is the "power of God" that saves, that keeps. We cannot for one moment keep ourselves. God must do it all. Christ in us is made unto us "wisdom, righteousness, sanctification and redemption." Would it not help many if they would think more of him, the Sanctifier, and having received him into their hearts, always recognize him as abiding there and as sufficient for all things?

Kept by the power of God, *through faith*. Nothing is received, nothing retained except through faith. It is faith that brings us near to God, faith that accepts the promises and makes them real, faith that enables one to get under the blood and to live in the fountain. All through faith! That soul that believes God, trusts him for all, walking in the light and keeping his commandments, shall be kept and presented blameless to the Father by the Savior at his coming.

It is conceded by those who are living in holiness that *direct testimony* is essential to the retaining of this experience. Paul commended Timothy for having made a good profession, and we read in Revelation, "They overcame him by the blood of the Lamb and the word of their testimony." The fact that so many have lost this grace by not testifying should tend to make one realize the importance of testimony.

In "Glimpses of Fifty Years" Frances E. Willard relates how she sought and obtained holiness, and was walking in the light of it when she was called to Lima Seminary in Western New York. After her arrival she was told by a minister in whom she had confidence and to whom she had related her experience, that it was good, but it would do much harm for her to profess it in that place, as certain people (referring to early Free Methodists) who were fanatical had rendered it unpopular. She heeded the advice, was silent on this subject, and as a result she says she lost at that time the witness and power of holiness.

God commands us to speak of his wondrous works and

to declare his glory and his great might. It seems only natural and right that to God should be given the glory of his wondrous works of grace as well as his other mighty acts.

The following passages— 1 Tim. 6:14; 1 Thess. 3:12, 13; 1 Thess. 5:23; 2 Pet. 3:11-14; 1 Jno. 2:28 and 1 Jno. 3:2, 3— show *the relation of this subject to the Second Coming of our Lord.* If we are looking for our Savior to come, how natural that it should increase in our hearts the desire to be always holy so as to be always ready. How much more difficult for the cares of the world to come in to choke the seed if one lives in constant expectation of the returning Master! How much less likely that the love of riches or the pride of life should creep in unawares if one expects so soon to be called to give an account of the entrusted talents! A hearty reception of the full truth as it is in Christ Jesus will greatly help one to retain, in and through Christ, that holiness which will render the possessor unashamed before the Lord when he shall come to judge and reward his servants.

Mrs. Emma Sellew Roberts, A.M.,
Associate Principal A.M. Chesbrough Seminary

"There is no Christian duty that has not been abused by inconsiderate, rash and weak minds. The same is true in the profession of justification. It can not be expected that the profession of holiness will be free from exhibitions of human frailty. The world is full of uncultivated, careless, rash, inconsiderate and impetuous men, and the profession of holiness, like all other Christian duties, is liable to abuse from them. Unwise professions of holiness, however, argue no more against its profession, than the abuse of prayer argues against the duty of prayer.

"There are some who profess holiness carelessly, and use objectionable and unguarded terms. These, in most cases, are those whose lives and spirit present but a sorry idea of Christian holiness. Such persons sometimes say, 'I am perfect,' 'I am pure,' 'I have not committed a sin for so long.' These things ought to be true, and may be true; but their careless utterance by some of the professed friends of holiness has done much to injure this precious doctrine, and bring its profession into disrepute. It was so in Mr. Wesley's day, and it is so in our day."

—*Wood's Perfect Love*

15
HOLINESS AS A STATE OF CHRISTIAN PERFECTION

CHRISTIANITY BEING A LIFE, it touches every part of our being, redeems each power, quickens all energies, and sanctifies every emotion. Mr. Wesley called Christian perfection the "second blessing," but did not teach that it was no more than a great blessing. As a synonym the term "second blessing" is misleading. Our feelings are not a reliable criterion by which to judge our spiritual standing. They necessarily variate, but the work wrought will remain. The emotions are manifold, while the state is one, and permanent. Selfishly to seek entire sanctification for the joy there is in it denotes the lack of pungent conviction, and results in superficiality and instability. Neither is pleasure nor the faculty by which we experience pleasure the supreme end of the Christian life. Some try to conjure themselves into special and ideal moods, instead of simply and bravely relying upon God's unshakable promises. Our emotions when sanctified have their legitimate place, but it is the condition of the heart that forms character, expresses person, and determines the immortal destiny of man.

We should distinguish between holiness as a state and the fruit of holiness, even as we would distinguish between the Holy Spirit and the "diversities of gifts" (1 Cor. 12:4), or between the Spirit and the "fruit of the Spirit" (Gal. 5:22, 23), or, again, between being "partakers of the divine nature" and the possession of the graces which are to be "added to our faith" (2 Peter 1:4-7). In each of the above instances there is a distinction, but in no instance are the state and fruit separable. As a state Christian perfection denotes a pure heart filled with perfect love; the abiding presence of the Comforter; delight in and oneness with the will of God; moral soundness, health, strength, stability, manhood. Hence it is a state of comparative maturity *plus ultra*.

The New Testament conception of Christian perfection is emphatic manliness: it is holy, puissant, self-centered, dauntless character. As an experience of consciousness it is characterized by changes; but as a state of moral purity and power it never fluctuates while the soul abides in Christ. The mental knowledge of our internal state is not always equally clear. There are physical, mental, and providential, as well as spiritual causes for the alternation of our sensibilities. Our space will not permit us to elaborate. There are periods when the emotions which accompany the Spirit are more vivid to the consciousness even of those who abide in Christ, than at other times. Thus under fresh illuminations of the Spirit joy may abound, and then again the soul will assume a more quiescent state. These fresh illuminations and unfoldings of the Spirit do not necessarily indicate that we have received a fresh baptism of the Spirit, nor that we need one when the soul assumes a state of quiet. Our love for and faith in God are no more to be estimated by such fluctuating tests than are our earthly loves and friendships. Spiritual ecstasies are mutable, while purity, love and faith may abide with an ever deepening tide, whether the flow be calm or excited, enabling us to abide in Christ and retain in ourselves the *abiding of the Holy Spirit.*

They who gauge their spiritual condition by their feelings are never quite sure of their whereabouts. The human life of Jesus, because of the conditions to which he subjected himself, was subject to many emotions, yet he laid no emphasis upon them. He was as pure when depressed as when exultant; when in the garden as when in the glory of the transfiguration. He never referred to these varied experiences as indicating any change in his character, or as effecting the great principle of his life. The important question is not, "How do you feel"? but "Is thine heart right"?

The design of grace is so to form the soul anew in holiness that immorality will be unnatural and practically impossible. The will of God and the ethical purpose of Scripture is, "the man of God," "a character with sinew of strength, and countenance of purity and courage." "All Scripture is given by inspiration of God that the *man* of God may be perfect." Permit me to give two illustrations, one of the permanency and the other of the solidity of this state, from the unadulterated Greek, which reveals the doctrine of Christian perfection clearer than the English version. In Matthew 11:28-30, the first word translated "rest" is *anapauo,* a verb which signifies "to refresh"; the second is *anapausin,* a noun signifying "a resting place." After being refreshed by the assurance of pardon and divine acceptance, which is the first rest, the convert should push right on, take the yoke and learn of Christ until the place or state of permanent repose is discovered, which is Jesus Christ, and there perpetually abide, undisturbed by the vicissitudes and turmoils of life. The second rest is to be immovable and lasting.

"Let us all in thee inherit,
Let us find that second rest."

Again, Jesus said to Peter, "I say unto thee that thou art Peter" (*Petros*, a piece of rock), a name denoting the solidity of his ultimate character. After Pentecost he was a rockman. Furthermore, through the reiterated smoothing and coloring of scene and sympathy divine, through the play and power of light and righteousness we may become, like Peter, not only a piece of rock, but "lively stones" (1 Peter 2:5); not stones just taken out of the quarry, natural rock, but *lithos*— the stone shaped, polished, ready for the building, of which Christ is the "chief corner stone" (*lithos*). Being "made perfect in love" we are to be "kept," "established," "settled," "rooted and grounded" therein.

There is opportunity for progress in the *state* of holiness. He that abides in Christ will have increasing perceptivity of mind in regard to spiritual things, increasing strength and stability, deepening experiences and enlargement of capacity. And while this glorious state is to be ascribed to the Holy Spirit, yet let us not forget that the "principle of virtue improved into a habit" (*Butler*)-a law unrepealed under grace which powerfully affects mind and body— has much to do (under the influence of the Spirit) with our establishment in holiness. Constant exercise in faith, prayer, watchfulness, holy meditation, and in the practice of Christian virtues tends to the formation of holy habits and to a fixed state of moral purity. Some are ever shifting, restless and inconstant, but "they that trust in the Lord shall be as mount Zion which cannot be removed, but abideth forever." Then trust not in your emotions, nor in circumstances; these may disappoint. To trust in the Lord is sanctified common sense. Repose in God. Behold the image of eternal steadfastness! the Mount which "sits to eternity," grappling with its rocky roots the earth's center; piercing with its highest pinnacle the furthest blue; which no storm can quiver, no earthquake shatter; changelessly uttering the changeless testimony, that faith in God is a settling and establishing virtue; that temptations and persecutions may menace, yet, believing, we are safe, in life, in death, and in eternity.

Blessed indeed is he who co-operates with God in making of himself "one new man." God the Father formed us; God the Son redeemed us; God the Holy Ghost regenerates and sanctifies us; manifold ministries test and develop us; and all to the end that we may "come unto a PERFECT MAN, unto the measure of the stature of the fullness of Christ."

Rev. Duane C. Johnson,
Of the Susquehanna Conference

16
Perfecting Holiness

GOD MADE MAN HOLY at his creation. Sin entered and marred the handiwork of God. The Lord did not, on that account, abandon the work of his own creation, but determined to defeat and destroy the work of the devil, and through redemption to bring forth in man the ideal character in which he was originally made, namely, "righteousness and true holiness". Not until our sanctification is entire, our holiness complete, therefore, will Jesus Christ "see [in us] the travail of his soul, and be satisfied". He has made provision to restore us to holiness. We are responsible for appropriating the provision he has made. Hence the admonition, based on exceeding great and precious promises, to "cleanse ourselves from all filthiness of the flesh and spirit, perfecting holiness in the fear of God."

The words, "perfecting holiness," may be understood to mean, *completing your sanctification*. By the work of cleansing here enjoined upon us our holiness will be made perfect. This is God's will concerning us. Yet many are afraid of this term perfect when applied to Christian character. They will throw up their hands in holy horror at the statement that a Christian may be made "perfect and complete in all the will of God," though the Bible positively enjoins it.

Doubtless some misapprehend the term, and suppose that to be a perfect Christian is to be equal to God himself. But the term is used in other senses than to denote absolute perfection. I call your attention to a violet, and tell you to "behold a perfect flower". You reply, "Sir, that flower is not perfect." I ask you, "Why not?" You begin to compare that tiny flower with a stately oak, and then remark to me, "Sir, that flower is not perfect; it is so much smaller than yonder oak that I cannot believe it is perfect." The plain answer would be, "The perfection of the flower is to be judged by a different standard from the perfection of the tree. It is not the nature of the violet to grow to such a stature and magnitude as the oak." Again, I point you to a horse, and say, "There is a perfect horse." You reply, "Impossible. That horse cannot talk, nor sing, nor reason, nor do many other things which a man can do. It cannot, then, be a perfect horse." I would have simply to remind you that the standards of perfection for the man and for the horse differ; and that the perfection of the horse is limited by the nature of the animal. I speak again of a Christian as being a perfect Christian and some one is ready to say, "What! Can he create a universe? Can he speak a world from naught? If he is perfect he must be possessed of all the attributes of Deity." I would answer, "Not so; to be a perfect Christian is to be perfect in that only which *constitutes* one a Christian. It is not to possess the perfections of Deity, nor to be perfect angels; but simply to be perfect in Christian character— "perfect and complete in all the will of God." This is the perfection or perfecting of holiness which is enjoined upon us in the scriptures. Our holiness is begun in regeneration; it is completed when we are wholly sanctified.

There is a sense, however, in which "perfecting holiness" should characterize the sanctified believer after the work of cleansing has been made complete; that is, *in the development and maturing of all the Christian graces.* Sanctification brings the soul into the best possible condition for growth in grace and for the development of the fruits of the Spirit. Growth should then be rapid. The soul's powers should expand, and the character and life should constantly exhibit an increasing conformity to the perfect model furnished by Jesus Christ.

The sanctified soul should also be constantly perfecting the *manifestation* of holiness. Many things render the manifestation of holiness quite imperfect in those who are wholly sanctified. Difference in temperament will effect a difference in the manifestation of spiritual life in two individuals equally holy. William Cowper was naturally despondent, and subject to attacks of melancholy. Some have charged it upon religion that he was so often and so greatly depressed. That is a sad mistake. Doubtless his religion was all that kept him from desperation and self-destruction at times. Cowper had grace, but grace did not change his physical temperament. There is a wide scope for Christians to exercise charity for one another on account of their differences in this respect. Some would naturally be light, buoyant and cheerful, even without saving grace; while others, with a high degree of spirituality, are of a turn of mind bordering on melancholy. We should beware of judging one another in these matters.

A man may be constitutionally quick, excitable, percussion-like. Let him experience entire sanctification, and it will not remold his constitution so as to make him like that other man who is so constituted that it would require something like an earthquake to startle him. After all sin is gone from his heart his constitutional peculiarity may remain, often leading others to misjudge him, and hindering the manifestation of God's work within him. Sanctification does not correct all the constitutional defects and infirmities in a day, nor in a year. The experience of sanctification, however, if retained, will gradually bring one to see the things that eclipse the manifestation of God's grace in his life, and enable him to overcome them. The manifestation of holiness will thus become more perfect by far after a score of years have been passed in the experience, than at the soul's first entrance into this blessed state.

REV. WILSON T. HOGG,
Editor of The Free Methodist

17
Holiness and the Ministry

THE FOUNDATION OF INFLUENCE and success in ministerial service is in the piety and spirituality of the ministry. Next to a divine call to the work, therefore, eminent piety is the most important qualification for the ministerial office. We say *eminent* piety, because ordinary religiousness will not meet the demand. Only superior spirituality and devotion can qualify one for such a holy calling.

Such are the nature and design of the ministerial office with its manifold duties that the Christian minister is regarded as pre-eminently a sacred man in society. He is looked up to as a model of moral excellence, and as one qualified by his own experience to lead his flock to exalted attainments in holiness. The people he serves have an unquestioned right, also, to expect in him a living example of that "holiness without which no man shall see the Lord." Moreover, the peculiar duties and responsibilities of his office are such as none but a holy man can adequately meet and fulfil. No man is prepared to go in and out before the flock of God as he should in the capacity of a Christian minister unless he can appeal to them as St. Paul did to the

Rev. Wilson Thomas Hogg

Thessalonian Christians when he said, "Ye are witnesses, and God also, how holily and justly and unblameably we behaved ourselves among you that believe" (1 Thes. 2:10).

The peculiar temptations incident to the work of the ministry also make it incumbent upon those who serve in the sacred office to be pre-eminently spiritual. "Nothing but the power and dominion of grace in a pure heart," says Rev. J. A. Wood, "can save any man from being affected in his ministerial work by his pocket-book, his reputation, or the frowns, the smiles, or the praise of men. It requires a pure heart and perfect love to be dead to all these things and to keep our 'eye single' and our 'whole body full of light.'" There are other and grosser though subtler forms of temptation, too, to which the minister is liable. They are met on the one hand in the discharge of those duties which sometimes necessitate his being made a confidant in matters of a private and delicate character; while on the other hand they may steal upon him under the plausible idea of cultivating spiritual communion. In either case the tendency is the same, namely, to occasion "turning the grace of God into lasciviousness." Into these snares many a once devoted and useful minister has been unwittingly drawn, thereby "making shipwreck of faith and a good conscience," and bringing reproach and disgrace upon the church of God. The best security against all those subtle and powerful temptations peculiar to the ministerial office is that of a pure heart— an experience of inward holiness. Above all others the Christian minister has need to "Put on the whole armor of God, that he may be able to stand against the wiles of the devil" (Eph. 6:11).

Conversion alone is not adequate to produce that depth, richness, fulness, and stability of Christian experience necessary to qualify one for the work of the ministry. In order to make full proof of his ministry the man who is called to this work should be *wholly sanctified*. We would not in any wise speak disparagingly of justification or of regeneration. To be born of God is a wonderful experience, and of itself makes one holy to the extent of imparting to his heart holy principles and giving them dominion over his life. This is not all that is included in holiness, however. It is holiness begun, but not holiness completed. Regeneration makes one a partaker of spiritual life; sanctification removes from the heart those native tendencies to sin which antagonize the development and full manifestation of that life. Regeneration gives power over inbred sin, and ability to conform the heart and life to the commands and precepts of the gospel; sanctification purifies or empties the heart of the principle of inbred sin, and prepares it for the personal, permanent indwelling of the Holy Spirit. Regeneration gives principles of holiness the ascendency [sic] over all carnal tendencies of the heart; sanctification annihilates those tendencies, swallowing up all carnal affections and dispositions in pure and perfect love, and leaving holiness to reign unrivalled and alone. To bring men into such a state as this is the grand aim of the gospel in all its provisions, promises, instructions and various ministries. How all-essential, then, that they who assume the responsibilities of the gospel ministry should be "holy men of God!" How necessary that they should be "pure in heart" and "perfect in love", as well as exemplary in outward life. How otherwise can they lead believers into that holiness which alone makes meet for efficient service on earth and for final admission into heaven?

Holiness is the chief element of success in the work of the ministry. It ranks above talents, learning, favorable circumstances, skilful management and ability in pulpit preparation and delivery. "Without it the minister can neither live, nor preach, nor labor as he should. There is a clearness, a strength, a fulness, an energy needed in the sacred office impossible without entire holiness. It would be infinitely better for the church and the world, if every partially sanctified minister would suspend all effort in other directions till, 'with strong crying and tears,' he receive the cleansing baptism of the Holy Ghost." —*Wood's Perfect Love.* "A thousand times as much stress ought to be laid upon this part of a thorough preparation for the ministry as has been," was President Finney's estimate of the case.

We can now see why the Savior forbade his chosen apostles to enter upon their public ministry until they had received the baptism of the Holy Ghost. They had been three years under his own instruction; they had been especially instructed in reference to their work; and they were assured that their names were written in heaven; still there was one indispensable qualification lacking. They needed to be "baptized with the Holy Ghost." Hence the command, "Tarry ye in the city of Jerusalem until ye be endued with power from on high," and the promise, "Ye shall receive power after that the Holy Ghost is come upon you." They tarried, and the promised baptism came. Then they were enabled to preach the gospel "in demonstration of the Spirit and of power," and thousands were converted and added to the church in a day as the result. Nothing short of this sanctifying baptism is adequate to produce an efficient ministry to-day.

Rev. Wilson T. Hogg,
Editor of The Free Methodist

18
HOLINESS THE POWER OF THE CHURCH

Holiness, IN ITS PERFECTED CHARACTER, is that deep and rich experience in which all sin is removed from the heart, every passion and power of the soul actuated by divine love and the entire being filled with the Holy Ghost. This, as experienced by individual Christians, we affirm to be the power of the church.

Mr. Webster defines the word power as "Ability to act... the faculty of doing or performing something... capability of producing an effect, whether physical or moral." The power of the church, then, is her faculty or capability of performing the work to which God has called her. The work of the church is that of saving sinners; not that of a reformatory. Her mission is not to refine the manners of society, nor to correct the conduct of the criminal classes, since these results will follow in her path of progress as a natural consequence; but her watchword is *salvation*. She sounds the tocsin against sin. Her heralds cry, "Repent and be converted. Life through Jesus Christ. Holiness and heaven." The power exercised by the church is delegated. It is derived from her relation to God, or by her full reception of

God's presence. This being true, it then stands to reason that every element or principle or passion in the church which is opposed to the reception of the Holy Spirit and which is antagonistic to his operations, must be removed if the church would exercise that full power which is essential to the accomplishment of her work. In the experience of holiness or entire sanctification this work is accomplished; *i.e.,* by the destruction of sin.

Sin opposes God. It is the only principle in regenerate man that antagonizes the Holy Spirit. When it can no longer reign it will rage; when dethroned by divine grace, it will stir up insurrection in the affections, until it is destroyed by the power of the atonement. "The flesh [sin] lusteth against the Spirit." "It is not subject to the law of God." It cannot be permanently suppressed. There is no law under heaven that can successfully regulate it. The Spirit is opposed in his leading, despised in his peace, rejected in his joy, and disputed in his authority by this monster, inbred sin.

Sin is a weakening element. Neither the intrigues of Satan, nor the ingenuity of men, nor the opposition of their combined forces can withstand a pure church. But an unsanctified church is a weak church. To arm a giant for battle is useless if he must needs walk with a cane and a crutch to war. Sin weakens the faith of the church; right in the heat of the conflict, fears arise, faith falters and the battle is lost. Sin chills the love of the church. We may substitute frenzy for fire, clamor for radical doctrines and insist on rigid rules of righteousness, but we only beat the air unless the soul of the church is fervent with divine love.

Sin is a blinding element. A man is of little use in war who cannot tell men from trees walking. A clear perception of truth and a right understanding of its application are essential in the work of the church. Obstacles are magnified, difficulties are doubled, dangers are increased, the face of God is obscured and heaven itself is sometimes uncertain when the vision of the soul is blurred by sin.

Sin is a distracting element. "In union there is strength" is never more true than when applied to the work of the church. The Apostle Paul declared the church at Corinth to be "carnal" because of their contention and division over favorite preachers. What havoc has been wrought in the church of God by sin as a contentious element! The dearest ties have been broken, societies severed, circuits divided, conferences rent in twain and whole organizations destroyed by a few who harbored sin. If the church succeeds she must maintain her unity of spirit and harmony of effort. If she does this she must insist upon holiness of heart in pulpit and pew.

Though the work of holiness accomplishes the utter extermination from the church of all the principles of opposition to her progress, this alone does not qualify her for her mission. The power of the church is not in negatives. A good road-bed and a clear track are essential to rapid train transit; but these may exist and the engine be dead on the track. The Spirit having accomplished this glorious work, the cleansing of the church, he then descends in all his fulness, inspiring, quickening and empowering her for her work. Now clad in armor omnipotent, invincible as her divine Master, she goes forth, heedless of earth's flatteries, unmoved by the world's frowns, reckless regarding her own temporal concerns, "fair as the moon, clear as the sun, and terrible as an army with banners." This heavenly unction was promised by Jesus to the lonely apostles as an enduement of power; and though the praying disciples understood not all that was contained in "the promise of the Father," they tarried until the rushing wind and the tongues of fire came which proved to be indeed a baptism of power. Superstition and prejudice were swept like chaff before the wind. Those whose hands were red with the blood of the world's Redeemer, and whose voices had so recently clamored for his condemnation, now cried in consternation at the fishermen's feet and prayed in penitence for mercy. In the presence of opposing priests, learned scribes and threatening tetrarchs, the disciples, under this baptism of power, soon "filled all Jerusalem with their doctrine." And from the day of this marvelous baptism on the infant church to the present time, the efficiency of the church in the accomplishment of her work has been in proportion to her reception of this heavenly unction.

History has confirmed, in all ages and nations, that the people who have enjoyed and taught the experience of Bible holiness, have been the ones who have forced their way through ignorance, superstition and idolatry, and planted the cross of Christ in the midst of misery, poverty and sin, and caused the desert to blossom as the rose.

If the church is thus to force her way through the fortifications of sin, and in the presence of Apollyon demand the liberty of his captives, she must have power to withstand the devil. Overtures to Satan are never successful. His open assaults, his secret devices, and his angels of light, make him a dreaded foe. She must also have power to resist the temptations of the world. How many moral giants have been slain by sin concealed in the soul which opened the door to temptation from without! More than one Sampson has lost his locks while dozing in Delilah's lap.

Again, she must have power to endure the persecutions of the world. To reprove the world for its sinful conduct and to denounce its carnal pleasures, is to incur its severest hatred and most bitter opposition. The enduement of power, which the church receives at the time of her perfect purification, fully qualifies her for this resistance and endurance. The aggressive power of the church lies in her ability to reach the hearts of men. To move the heart of the world, the heart of the church must first throb. Holiness creates in the church a consuming concern for the lost. Her ministers lose their second-hand sermons, and revamped discourses and break right out from the heart in declarations of truth, born by inspiration, amid the flaming affections of the soul. Men are more than moderately moved by such truths. The agitation is more than mental. Daniel Webster said, after hearing a young man preach, "That young man is evidently an unscientific man, but he has gone to the school of God and knows some things of which I am ignorant. I have had my intellect entertained by other ministers, but that young man has touched my heart."

The power of the church is not demonstrated alone by a sanctified ministry. There must be harmony existing between the character and conduct of the church, and the teaching of her pulpits. The testimony and example of a holy church are sometimes more powerful than her pulpits. Many hearts that have proven too hard for the pulpit hammer have yielded to the tears and testimony of the pew. Others who have rejected both sermons and testimonies have been forced to their knees by the silent suffering and shining faces of the saints of God, who have died in the flames of burning fagots with prayers on their lips for their murderers.

We observe, then, from the foregoing, whether considered from the philosophical relations of inbred sin to the work of the church, or from the provisions of grace and the promise of God; or from the history of the church, whether considered in her aggressive attitude or that of resistance and suffering, that the power of the church in the accomplishment of her work depends upon her attaining unto the experience of entire holiness.

Rev. F.D. Brooke,
Of the Illinois Conference

19
Preaching Holiness

1. *H*AVE IT. DRINK IT, inhale it, bathe in it, live in it and let it live in you, until you breathe it out as naturally as Saul of Tarsus breathed out threatenings and slaughter. This is the first, indispensable qualification for preaching either entire sanctification or justification. St. Augustine's "Confessions" have stirred the souls of thousands for fifteen centuries because of the divine reality in them. Whatever we may think of much else in them, we cannot but be moved at the account of his mother's years of prayer and patience, his wanderings, his ambition, his sins, his remorse, his desperate struggle, the strange providence that sealed his resolution and his faith, his companion joining him, and his mother leaping and praising God and not long after joyfully dying, content to be buried in a strange land because she felt her work was done. The influence of Augustine for good has lived until this day because of the divine life which entered his soul in that garden in Italy so many centuries ago.

John Tauler lived two hundred years before the Reformation, in the period when the Black Death smote the world, and during the night of Papal domination, but salvation made him a flame of fire. Under his preaching of three experiences,— nature, grace, and the direct shining of the Holy Spirit,— many fell strengthless, and Strasburg and Germany were shaken by a power which, through Tauler's writings and otherwise, is felt through the world to this day. The "Imitation of Christ" was written by a Roman Catholic, long before the days of Luther, but it contains an experience that has preached to the world in more editions than any other book except the Bible.

Let us, as far as possible, have sound theology, but first let us have the indwelling Christ. Better would it be to have the life in God enjoyed by a Thomas á Kempis, even though we believed in transubstantiation, and the life enjoyed by Bunyan, even though we were advocates of Calvin's "horrible decree," than to be as clear as crystal in the doctrine of holiness, while as cold as ice, or as grasping as Nabal, or as frothy as yeast and as unreliable as quicksand. Real experience has a tongue of fire and will almost literally repeat the miracle of Pentecost. Brother Paul,— Masazi Murahashi,— who lately left us for Japan, was not a fluent speaker in English, and some things in Binney's Compend were a puzzle to him; but it was a hard heart indeed that would not melt to hear him tell of his conversion in Japan, his persecutions, his shipwreck, his floating "in middle ocean" holding to a plank while the waves rolled over him, and how that then, though he had not heard entire sanctification preached, he felt he needed before he died the experience taught in the hymn he had learned, "Now wash me, and I shall be whiter than snow," and how he prayed for it and it came so that he waved one hand and shouted.

2. *Preach it with the Holy Ghost.* We are sanctified by the Spirit, and only by his help can effectual preaching be done. Without him holiness doctrine and profession are as an engine without fire or steam, or a body without a soul.

We must continually be on our guard at this point, for the tendency with ecclesiastical organizations has always been sooner or later practically to substitute something else in religion for a present, living God. The thing substituted may or may not be something good in its own place, but even though it were the Jewish temple and its ceremonial, or though it should be education, culture, ritualism or orthodoxy in holiness, if it is allowed to rob us of the baptism and indwelling of the Holy Ghost it has accomplished the design of Satan. Daily communion with God and repeated incomings of power from on high are the only security against apostasy for either preacher or people. With this, the weakest are strong; without it, the mightiest are broken reeds, piercing those who lean upon them.

3. *Preach it in its completeness*. It should be set forth in all its relations, phases, applications. To do this, no cast-iron regulations can be laid down to suit every occasion. Much, very much dependence must be placed in the Spirit, for direction as to the specific thing or things to be emphasized on particular occasions. Sir William Hamilton is reported to have called President Finney the strongest intellect of this century, yet Mr. Finney put the utmost stress upon being directed and helped by the Spirit in preaching.

The preaching of holiness should be as broad and as varied as the Bible; hence the "daily, nightly, and everlasting study" of the Bible is indispensable. To neglect this for newspapers and current literature will prove fatal to real and abiding success. No unvarying rule as to the mode of studying it can be laid down for every one, nor for the same person at all times, but the servant of Christ must love his Bible more than a novel reader loves a novel, a historian an ancient chronicle, or a scientist the book of a master. If this love is wanting, it must be sought, obtained and cherished.

4. *Read the best books*. Spurgeon said that he never tired

reading the sermons of men who had been eminently successful in winning souls. This was one of his habits that will well bear imitation. Spiritual biographies are a power in helping a preacher.

"The wise new wisdom from the wise acquire,
And each bold hero lights another's fire."

Each new acquaintance thus formed is a rich and an abiding acquisition and inspiration. There is an inexpressible delight in such reading, unspeakably above that furnished by any novel, and it benefits the reader, makes him more useful, and doubtless gives him a foretaste of the closer, wider acquaintanceships to be formed in heaven.

But we must close. The theme is boundless and exhaustless. Without continual fellowship with God, no one is qualified to preach holiness. Of himself no one is ever sufficient, but he who knew the secrets of the sea of Galilee and who knows the hearts of men and all depths, has said: "Follow me, and I will make you fishers of men."

Rev. John La Due,
Instructor in Hebrew, Greenville College

20
MEETINGS FOR HOLINESS

B<small>Y MEETINGS FOR HOLINESS</small> I do not mean holiness conventions or camp-meetings, but regular meetings in connection with the work of the Lord in the same order as class or weekly prayer meetings. It has been my privilege to be where they were held with very favorable results.

The first meetings of this kind that I ever attended were in connection with my school days. Some of the students adopted the plan of having a meeting for holiness every Sabbath morning at 5 a. m., in the fall and spring terms, and at 5:30 o'clock in the winter term. The meetings were conducted entirely by students. I do not remember any teacher being present during the period of over two years that I was there as a student, but the Lord used to meet with us and bless us and keep us alive in the midst of spiritual dearth.

After my school days were ended and my surroundings changed I used to long for such select meetings for believers and seekers, but never found them again till we moved to Binghamton, N.Y. There we found that a meeting for holiness was one of the established weekly meetings of the church. Monday evening was the one set apart for this purpose. It is impossible for me to give anything like a correct report of the amount of good accomplished at these meetings. It was here the tried and tempted believer found help. The young converts were made strong as they were led on unto perfection, and convicted sinners were converted. Sometimes the sick were healed in answer to the prayer of faith. It was here that the cause of truth and righteousness in Binghamton was established. Oh, how the blessed Spirit was poured out at times upon the humble few who took the narrow way from choice! We spent five years in Binghamton when my husband was first appointed pastor, and some years afterward he served two more as pastor and one as district chairman; but all this time the Monday evening meeting continued with interest and profit, and I do not know but it still continues. Thank the Lord for those precious seasons of refreshing.

When we left Binghamton for other fields of labor we were both better acquainted with God than when we went there, and this is saying but little of the benefits realized in those Monday night meetings. It seemed to me very much like a theological school.

In the different fields of labor that followed we found no meetings for holiness established. My soul was often hungry for such seasons with God's people. When we came to Dakota, ten years since, we found a good degree of interest in the subject of holiness in different places, but no meetings established especially for its promotion. Early morning prayer meetings were usually held in connection with the camp-meetings, the same as in the East, with more or less of divine help. It was not until the fifth year after we came here that it was decided by those in authority that the early prayer meeting should assume a definite character, having as its object the promotion of scriptural holiness as believed by Wesley and his followers. This plan has continued ever since its adoption; and, as the result, the number of witnesses to the experience of entire sanctification has been largely increased. Praise the Lord. Ever since we have been living at Wessington Springs I have felt a strong desire for an old-type holiness meeting. Some have been held, but not regularly until last year, when it seemed clear that the time had come to establish such meetings. They are now held regularly every Sabbath afternoon and are seasons of special blessing and profit to those who attend.

As Free Methodists we profess to believe in entire holiness, or sanctification, as a distinct work wrought in the soul subsequent to justification. We promised when we were received into the Free Methodist Church in full connection that, if we were not then in the enjoyment of this state, we would seek until we found. Have we all kept our vows? Dear reader, have you gone on to perfection, and do you now realize that the blood of Jesus cleanses your heart from all unrighteousness? and does the Holy Ghost fill your soul? We must have this grace ourselves, or we cannot fulfil our mission, which is to spread scriptural holiness over these lands. Much help will be realized all through the church, I fully believe, by having special meetings for holiness.

Mrs. M.H. Freeland,
Wessington Springs, S.D.

21
HOLINESS AND REFORMS

THAT GODLINESS IS THE SOURCE of reform passes without saying among all classes who acknowledge the power of Christianity. That sin is the seat of trouble is demonstrable. Blunders which have ruined churches, paralyzed business, and destroyed empires may be traced to dark original sin more easily than hunters would follow the trail of a fox to his lair. For the blighting effect of sin is never effaced. How much more apparently does deliberate sinning add to this fount of pollution, sending forth its pestilential streams of selfish interest, from which rise the blighting miasmas of greed and the lust of power!

The world is silently witnessing the death struggle of Labor with the terrible grip of Capital upon its throat. It is the aristocracy of the few triumphing over the humanity of the many,— revealing the poor, the widow and the fatherless trodden under the iron heel of a purely moneyed despotism. To find the remedy is easy; successfully to apply it involves the principle of holiness. Surely, then, it cannot be done by the men of the world who represent the various industries. Blinded by selfish interest— the god of this world— each makes himself a central sun, regarding others merely as satellites to revolve about him. The history of astronomy affords a striking illustration of the only way out of the difficulty. The first astronomers, like our average business men, supposed that this little earth,— really one of the smallest of only one small planetary system,— was the center of the universe. But somehow their calculations of celestial movements, like the bank account of our business men who want to be suns, would never come out right. Finally one astronomer made a bold departure from the theories and philosophies of his predecessors. Leaving the earth, he took his position by the sun. To his astonishment and joy his calculations now came out exactly right— especially after substituting one of the two foci for a common center. Each planet completed its orbit at the very moment he had calculated for it. Kepler had found the key to astronomical science. The greatness of his discovery struck him with strange power. The universe suddenly appeared so inconceivably grand, its vastness so great, yet its movements marked by such hair-breadth precision, that he sank to the ground overwhelmed. There is an eternal SUN in our heavens the white light of whose shining is his own increate essence— HOLINESS UNTO THE LORD. Wherever admitted this Light of Life is all-pervading, all-controlling. The time may be when earth, awaking from slumber shall acknowledge his reign as the angels do, thus spanning earth and heaven with this bow of promise: "In that day shall there be upon the bells of the horses, HOLINESS UNTO THE LORD; and the pots in the Lord's house shall be like the bowls before the altar. Yea, every pot in Jerusalem and in Judah shall be holiness unto the Lord of hosts" (Zech. 14:20, 21).

This much-desired time evidently is not yet. Closely following the dark reign of injustice and tyranny is the prowling monster of open vice. Where is our good Anthony

Comstock? and where are his many self-proclaimed coadjutors? The air is filled with sheets reeking with bawdy pictures. In defiance of all honor and decency our buildings and fences are placarded with monstrous posters in which the very devil seems to be outdoing himself. All this moral filth is the natural outgrowth of legalized prostitution. William T. Stead, who wrote, "If Christ Came to Chicago," has been roughly handled, even by good Christians, because, as it seems to us, he was about fifty years ahead of his time. We believe time will demonstrate that he struck a ringing blow of gospel truth against the bulwarks of hell when he declared that the vices of the American people largely lay at the doors of American churches. Why, there are men in Joliet penitentiary to-day for embezzling funds to enable their wives and daughters to maintain that position in society which they had chosen, and, too, within the pale of an orthodox denomination. Furthermore,— and let not this shock you,— there are girls standing this moment behind the curtained pane in the many entrance doors to perdition lining Fourth avenue, among the comparatively few who failed to conceal their shame incurred by multitudes for a similar purpose. A general house-cleaning in the temple of God, pushed vigorously on until HOLINESS once more flashes forth from the altar behind the vail, would accomplish more toward putting down crime and prostitution than would all other combined agencies.

Some reforms are threadbare, while others, equally or more important, are scarcely touched. We believe that the evils of secret, oath-bound societies are not sufficiently ventilated by the pulpit and press of this country. The abduction and murder of Captain William Morgan, and the popular agitation that followed, causing a general collapse of Freemasonry for more than a quarter of a century, are still fresh in the minds of the fathers. But time heals all wounds, and we are given to understand by the knowing ones that the whole thing is a myth springing from the fertile brain of anti-Masons. Before me lies a quarto volume of Lippincott's Pronouncing Biographical Dictionary, brought down to 1887. On page 1767 we read: "*Morgan* (William), an American mechanic, born in Virginia about 1775, removed subsequently to Batavia, New York. In 1826 he was abducted and murdered by a band of Freemasons for having written a book professing to disclose the secrets of their society. (*See 'Allen,' 'American Biographical Dictionary;' 'New American Encyclopædia;' 'Gazetteer of the State of New York,' by J. H. French, p. 323."*)

Courts of justice, powerless under the fatal charm of the hoodwink and cabletow which more than once have paralyzed the executive functions of our very government, proclaim Freemasonry to be a stupendous monopoly of rights and privileges belonging to all. By her own minions has it often been shown to the world as an institution of organized selfishness. To say that any body of men has a more sacred right to "life, liberty and the pursuit of happiness" than have the rest of mankind is to affirm what every loyal American citizen knows to be a lie. Yet this is precisely the sort of lying which composes the (ig)"noble" structure of Freemasonry. Let anyone doubting this statement send ten cents to the National Christian Association, 221 West Madison street, Chicago, for authorized "light" on the subject. This would be far cheaper and far more honorable than to stumble blindfolded for "light" through the horrible Masonic labyrinth of blood-curdling oaths and blasphemies.

Freemasonry is usually selected as the principal target of reform guns because she is the recognized mother of the numerous brood of secret orders which are filling the land. Drive out this mother of villianies [sic] and her progeny must follow. Many hoped that the public airing of secret fraternities which Dr. Cronin's murder furnished the world would disrupt not only the infamous Clan-na-Gael but the whole pestiferous brood of secret clans. But secretists were taught a lesson by the landslide that struck them when they killed Morgan,— and now "all's quiet." A few years hence it may be doubted whether such a man as Dr. Cronin ever existed; and people who are anxious to know may have to consult our court records.

The feature of secret institutions that most interests us at present is their religious character. Who has not witnessed the mock solemnities of a Masonic funeral and the appalling blasphemy of sending the soul of the departed, whether drunkard or knave, to the "Grand Lodge above," by upraised hands of the fraternity around the open grave at the word of command from the "Worshipful Master"? Anyone can find further and abundant proofs that Freemasonry is a religion from the published works of Masonic authorities (Address the N.C.A. as above). As all secret orders either directly or indirectly antagonize the Bible— the proofs of which abound for those who care to know— their religion must be a FALSE one. As a matter of fact it constitutes an armament of false worship whose forces are consolidated against the religion of Jesus Christ. A determined collision between the two must inevitably follow; because, on the other hand, true religion always aims her artillery at false systems. Holiness, therefore, in both its germ and fruition, is the mighty God-power to pull down this stronghold of Satan. All other agencies of reform are futile as compared with this. Indeed, to attempt anything in this direction without it were only to beat the air. False religion must be conquered by true religion, if conquered at all. The sooner our anti-secret reformers discover this truth, and practically utilize it, the better will it be for them and for the laudable work which they have undertaken.

The curse of intemperance is too commonly distributed among three classes— distillers, venders and consumers of ardent spirits. We are prohibitionists, but fear we are fighting King Alcohol in the dark. Sojourning in Chicago has opened our eyes somewhat. "Family beer" wagons may often be seen before the well-known residences of church members; and later on these same "family beer" wagons and "lager beer" wagons may be seen side by side at breweries and wholesale beer houses. The same stuff goes into both. One goes to the church members, the other to the saloons. Chicago is a city not likely to wipe out the saloons while her good church-member citizens conduct themselves after such a fashion. But she can easily do this if she thinks she must. Grade- crossings were backed by the mightiest corporations on earth,— but Chicago spoke, and, at enormous expense, they raised their tracks. Gambling represents the supreme interest of some of the heaviest capitalists on the continent. As often as Chicago has spoken gambling has ceased. So we have reason to know that she can, if she will, close every saloon in town. And we have reason to further know that if every church member in the city did but use his utmost influence and vote in that direction Chicago would soon be brought to the point where she would be glad to take hold of the saloon business— AND STOP IT! To prove this by simple statistical showings would consume more space than at present is allotted to us.

Where, then, lies the greatest burden of responsibility touching the temperance question? The manufacturer, the middle man and the vender are blinded by their unholy gains. The degree of responsibility is determined, first, by one's convictions; second, by his freedom to act. In a general sense all wrong doers are responsible— the heathen themselves being without excuse according to Saint Paul. But greater responsibility attaches to those who sin with their eyes wide open— who profess to be serving God while serving the world, the flesh and the devil. The responsibility of these is of such enormous proportions as to bury that of others almost out of sight. Then the opportunities within one's reach largely determine his responsibility. What class now do you think is most responsible for the curse of intemperance? Is it not the church member? He believes, at least abstractly, in holiness. Did he enjoy what he professes to believe what a general capsize would there be in all moral conditions! How quickly would the gigantic structure of wrong begin to totter to its eternal fall, whose welcome crash would herald the oncoming millennium: while true Christianity, "as the wings of a dove covered with silver, and her feathers with yellow gold" (Psa. 68:13), would rise, Phœnix-like, from the ashes and "pots" among which she has so long lain. Lord, hasten the glad hour. Hasten it by clothing Zion with her emblem of divine power— TRUE HOLINESS.

Rev. Charles H. Rawson, A.M.,
Editor of the Sunday-School Weekly

22
Practical Holiness

AMONG THE DEFINITIONS GIVEN in the "Standard Dictionary" to the word *practical* are these: "1. Pertaining to or governed by actual use and experience as contrasted with ideals and speculations... 5. Manifested in practice; as *practical* religion. 'The soul of religion is the *practical* part.' — *Bunyan Pilgrim's Progress.*" Viewed in the light of these definitions I conclude that "practical holiness" is holiness reduced to or manifested in practice.

Men without grace may touch many points of practical godliness; but however moral or well trained in the theory of right conduct, without an experimental knowledge of God and having never been born of the Spirit, they will signally fail in other points. The unregenerate heart will manifest its nature somewhere— and quite probably when one is least aware of the manifestation. Similarly the converted man may have dominion over sin and his conduct may usually appear to run in a line parallel with that of the one who has been "sanctified wholly;" but ever and anon he is liable to be surprised into some method of procedure or some act which is unholy. The carnal nature is bound to assert itself. In order to manifest holiness, always, under all circumstances, the theory must be realized in experience. The soul must reach out beyond accepted theoretical statement and belief into a heart experience. This experience is the beginning of practical holiness.

Having been made holy, having professed the grace of sanctification, his family, the church, the world, and all who mingle with the man expect and have a right to expect that his daily life will be a manifestation of practical holiness.

Practical holiness will regulate *domestic life*. The husband who has this experience will find that its practical manifestation controls each item of his every-day life. His treatment of his wife, his regard for her comfort and her wishes and his constant love for her will be measured by the apostle's direction, "Husbands, love your wives even as Christ also loved the church, and gave himself for it," etc. (Eph. 5:25-28). The rule, "So ought men to love their wives as their own bodies," if practiced, would often remodel the whole of family life. There is no room here for harshness, for coarseness, for sensuality. The one who loves his wife as Christ loved the church will be a holy man in his home life, and this experience will sanctify every relation and phase of the God-ordained institution of marriage. It is almost unnecessary to state that a like practical manifestation of holiness should and will mark the life of the sanctified woman. She will be the "virtuous woman" Solomon describes "whose price is far above rubies"; she will stretch "out her hand to the poor," and reach "forth her hands to the needy," and the "heart of her husband" may "safely trust in her." From homes in which all hearts are thus controlled by practical holiness would spring a race of beings purer, nobler, and more susceptible of culture— physical, mental and spiritual— than any the world has seen in later years. Practical holiness would give to the world children who were "well born," capable of grand attainments and destined for grand achievements.

Practical holiness reaches *political life*. It causes the one possessing the experience to vote like a Christian. He does not cringe to public sentiment, curry public favor, nor sell himself for political preferment. It divorces him from all tricky schemes which characterize almost every phase of political life. Holiness carried into the political life of the nation would cure the evils which now render a large majority of our population miserable and degraded. But if its universal manifestation were an event to be looked for only with the advent of the millennium, still the obligation of the individual Christian would remain to be holy in heart and to evince in his contact with the political world, in every case, that practical holiness which should be the concomitant of the inward experience.

Practical holiness extends to every phase of *business life*. It has to do with men's dealings with others. It buys, sells and bargains by the Golden Rule— "All things whatsoever ye would that men should do to you," etc. The man who saw the fine points of two young animals which a poor man in close circumstances solicited him to purchase, apprised their owner of their prospective value, advised him to keep them and loaned him money to carry him through his strait, instead of profiting by his neighbor's ignorance and necessity, gave a practical exhibition of holiness that carried out in every-day life would prevent the few from becoming vastly wealthy and put the many in circumstances of temporal comfort.

Practical holiness *in social life* is the ultimate and radical cure for talebearing, slander, evil speaking, etc. It will never take up a reproach against another. The late Rev. Joseph Travis once wrote: "It is bad enough if my neighbor has a reproach without my taking it up and carrying it to others." That a thing is true does not justify one in repeating it, if thereby another will be injured in his reputation; for reputation is more valuable than gold. Treasure may be replaced, but a reputation once soiled is rarely brightened again. Practical holiness, then, is exhibited by a sanctified tongue.

Holiness practically manifested controls every department of *church life*. It is felt in the official board, the quarterly conference, the annual conference, the general conference; and one of the grandest manifestations of practical holiness may be made in the "church trial." The official boards whose members have holy hearts transact business to the glory of God. The conferences where holiness is the experience of the members are free from all methods resorted to by unholy politicians. Holy men do not trade their votes in conference for their own advancement or honor. They never bargain to give so many votes for a certain man for a desired position if that man will vote for another for some other coveted preferment. Holy men do not influence whole delegations to attain certain ends as do unprincipled men of the world. Holiness practiced makes the convocations of religious bodies holy convocations.

In the church trial (for such things must occur sometimes while all men are human and some carnal) practical holiness insures the telling of the accused his fault first privately. If he does not hear the one, it takes two or three to endeavor if possible to "restore such an one in the spirit of meekness." It makes the final trial a last resort, and labors to ascertain the truth rather than to expel the accused as a result of unsanctified envy or prejudice. A practical manifestation of holiness in dealing with accused persons might have saved many a church member to a life of usefulness and caused many a minister to continue to make full proof of his ministry. Practical holiness restores and saves the offender, if possible, preferring such a result to sacrificing the accused. It loves souls as well as it regards the reputation of the church.

It may be urged as an objection that many who profess,

and doubtless many who possess the experience of holiness do not, in all cases, measure up to the standard of practical holiness. This is no doubt true. Limited knowledge and the failure of the religious press and the pulpit to proclaim the truth will account for much of this failure in practice. It is our duty to declare the truth. Its declaration will cause men to think, to reflect, to examine the word, and to seek in prayer and by self-examination to "perfect holiness in the fear of God"; that finally a tidal wave of holiness, experienced and manifested, may "turn many to righteousness" and bring many sons to the glory world.

Let us seek to be holy in heart and life. Let us enjoy and illustrate Bible holiness uniformly and constantly.

Mrs. Mary C. Baker,
Office Editor of the Free Methodist

23
Spurious Holiness

The present is an age of shams, of superficiality, of counterfeits, of adulterations, of admixtures, in almost every department of life. Nor is the religious world free from them. Only that which is valuable is worth counterfeiting. In proportion to the value of an article is the effort made to produce its counterfeit. There are many phases of religious profession that the devil does not care to imitate. They are so worthless he has no need to substitute anything in their place. It cannot be denied he accomplishes much harm by the principle of substitution, by offering the sham for the real, the shoddy for the good. It is lamentable that he finds such a trade for his wares, that so many will accept his imitations and reject the genuine.

The experience of true holiness is glorious. It ushers us into sacred nearness to God. It gives a gracious sense of purity to the soul. It destroys the carnality of our hearts. It lifts us far above the iniquities of the sinful world, the pleasures of sin, and the vain ambitions of this life. It gives strength in time of temptation, and consolation in time of grief. It alone can fit us to die and prepare us to enter the city of God. No wonder the devil would try to deceive us in reference to this experience.

The Lord warns us against the false by exhorting us to obtain the real. "That ye put on the new man, which after God is created in righteousness and true holiness." In these days it has become popular to preach and to profess holiness. But we fear in many cases it is not the Bible kind. Pity is it that so much of the false, and so little of the true, should be taught and professed.

Within the limits of this article we desire to call attention to some phases of spurious holiness.

1. Spurious holiness is often founded upon wrong conceptions of the doctrine of justification. Our belief always affects our character and our life. There are holiness leaders who teach that holiness alone delivers from actual sin. Very many accept this erroneous doctrine and profess to be entirely sanctified when in reality they are only justified. Their teaching and example causes others to live in the commission of known sin and at the same time profess to be converted. A preacher once made the statement from the pulpit that Mr. Wesley had a sermon on "sinning Christians." He doubtless referred to the sermon entitled "Sin in Believers," but utterly failed to distinguish between the two statements. In harmony with such spurious teaching concerning holiness, we have often heard professors of religion, when reproved for dressing like the world, using tobacco, getting angry, attending balls and theatres, and such like things, reply, by way of self-justification, "We do not profess holiness." To make room for their theory of holiness, they minify conversion until it becomes too small to be seen and too powerless to be of any good. I believe that, as far as our outward deportment is concerned, we are required to live just as correctly, and walk as circumspectly, by the standard of justification as by that of entire sanctification.

2. That holiness is spurious which is not deeply interested in the conversion of sinners. Much of the holiness of to-day consists in having a good time, in seeking "baptisms of power," in hiding in some corner away from contact with the world and "getting blest." It knows nothing about travail of soul for sinners, does not go into the highways and hedges seeking the lost, does not offer a helping hand to the needy and oppressed. It is the "goody-goody" kind, that agrees with everything and everybody and offends none. It trims its sails to catch the favoring breezes. It has no opposition, no persecution, no trial, no conflict, and it begets no souls.

3. It is a spurious holiness that lives in conformity to the world in dress, in business, or in politics. In these matters the plain word of God is disregarded. "Be not conformed to the world, but be ye transformed by the renewing of your mind," "Love not the world, neither the things which are in the world," and other passages of similar import, are trampled upon or explained so as to mean but little. It is very common nowadays for persons to profess holiness while their attire plainly shows they have not renounced worldly fashion. Men wearing costly and showy ornaments of gold, and women clad in the latest style of fashion, bear testimony, or pose as leaders of what they term the "higher life." The Scriptural injunction: "I will that men pray everywhere, lifting up holy hands, without wrath or doubting. In like manner, also, that women adorn themselves in modest apparel, with shamefacedness and sobriety, not with broidered hair, or gold, or pearls, or costly array," seems to be a dead letter.

In business life they adhere to the worldly principles, shave notes at heavy discount, charge exorbitant interest, drive sharp bargains, look out for what they call "number one," consider not the interests of their neighbors, and leave the impression upon the unsaved that they are seeking the almighty dollar rather than serving Almighty God.

In politics allegiance to party seems dearer than allegiance to Jesus Christ and his principles. They give their influence to put men in office who are corrupt and to measures which are a disgrace to our civilization. They may sing temperance songs, offer temperance prayers, and preach temperance sermons, but they go to the ballot box and vote for the continuation of the rum traffic. Surely the holiness that ignores Bible principles in dress, in business relations and in politics, is spurious.

4. It is a spurious holiness that believes a person can be right with God while he ignores the just claims of his fellow-men. There are those who profess holiness and go into raptures over the prospects of getting to heaven, who do not render to their neighbors their due. Some of them give large sums to endow colleges, to build churches, to establish missions, to send the gospel to the heathen, to support the preaching at home, to sustain benevolent enterprises. But this very money has been obtained by oppressing the poor, by robbing the widow, by grinding their workmen down to long hours and starvation wages. True holiness requires that men shall be just, as well as generous. If the workmen got more, and the church less, of this money, evidently the Lord would be better pleased with the transaction. It is one of the most damnable delusions that men can deal unjustly with their fellow-men, and, because of their liberality to God's cause, can get a passport to glory. Giving to the Lord's work will never atone for the injustice and oppression wrought upon poor humanity. Concerning this the Lord has spoken as follows: "I will come near to you to judgment, and I will be a swift witness against… those that oppress the hireling in his wages, the widow, and the fatherless, and that turn aside the stranger from his right" (Mal. 3:5). "He that oppresseth the poor to increase his riches shall surely come to want (Prov. 22:16).

5. It is a spurious holiness that countenances and supports worldliness and worldly measures in the church. The

majority of the churches make use of means to raise money which are plainly at variance with the principles of the Bible. The mere mention of some of these devices is enough to make a heathen turn away in disgust. Fairs, festivals, grab-bags, neck-tie parties, apron bazars [sic], dog shows, donkey socials, shadow parties, masquerades, second-class theatres, gymnastic performances, and many other kinds of nonsense— all in the name and for the benefit of the church,— must make the angels weep, and directly tend to delude and damn souls. Many of these are given by churches which declare they have been raised up "to spread scriptural holiness over these lands." Holiness professors either attend and take part in these schemes or support the churches that make use of them. It is very significant that Christ's first act in his public ministry, and also one of his very last public acts prior to his crucifixion, was to cleanse the temple of the unholy traffic in merchandise, and stamp his condemnation upon those who thus desecrated the sacred place.

6. That holiness which will allow persons to adhere to secret societies is spurious. The Bible demands our separation from unbelievers. Secrecy unites the just and the unjust, believers and sinners, the preacher and the libertine, in one bond of fellowship; united by oaths forbidden by the word of God; united by principles of the most intense selfishness the world ever saw. True holiness is open and free and benevolent. Secrecy works in the dark and is so clannish that it regards none but its own adherents in its ministrations of pretended charity. Christianity teaches that all men are brothers. Secrecy limits its obligations to those who have taken its blood-curdling oaths and sworn allegiance to its mandates. It robs the church of the proper service of her members and puts a spiritual blight upon those who associate in its councils. Some lodges deny the name of the Lord Jesus Christ a place in their ritual and in their prayers, and most of them deny the principles which

he taught. At the threshold of every lodge in the land, in the promise of secrecy, persons are required to violate plain commandments of the Bible. It is written: "If a soul swear, pronouncing with his lips to do evil, or to do good, whatsoever a man shall pronounce with an oath, and it be hid from him; when he knoweth of it, then he shall be guilty in one of these" (Lev. 5:4), Such a person was required to offer a sin offering for his trespass that he might secure pardon. Yet professed Christian ministers and holiness teachers and professors are numbered among this selfish clan, and the holy cause of Jehovah is dishonored and robbed of its glory.

7. That holiness which does not manifest the spirit of Jesus Christ before the world is spurious. Jesus was humble. He said, "Learn of me, for I am meek and lowly in heart, and ye shall find rest unto your souls." Many of these professors are proud. Jesus was unworldly. He declared his followers were not of this world. Many of these are worldly in the extreme and are floating along with the terrible tide that is ruining the church. Jesus was unselfish. He lived for others. These live lives of selfishness and know but little of self-denial for Christ's sake. Jesus, when reviled, reviled not again. These get angry when opposed, resent injuries, are impatient under trial, fret under reverses, give way under temptation, and show but little of the kind, loving, tender, forgiving spirit of their Master. Genuine holiness enables us to be patient toward all men, kind and considerate, tender and forgiving. It keeps us unruffled when abused, helps us to render good for evil, and in all the relations of life enables us to manifest the divine, instead of the carnal, nature. It is our duty to have Christ for our example. The word is plain. "Let this mind be in you which was also in Christ Jesus" (Phil. 2:5). "He that saith he abideth in him, ought himself also so to walk even as he walked" (1 John 2:6). "Christ also suffered for us, leaving us an example that ye should follow his steps" (1 Peter 2:21). The votaries

of spurious holiness pattern after an ungodly world that crucified the Son of God. Such holiness is a sham, a delusion, and a snare.

The day of reckoning draws nigh. That which is not founded upon the truth must go down. In the final determinations of the last day, all that is spurious shall be consigned to the realm of perpetual night, while the true shall enter into the regions of Eternal Day.

Rev. J.T. Logan,
New York Conference

Since writing the above, I have read some of Brother B. T. Roberts' articles, compiled under the title of "Holiness Teachings." I beg leave to add the following notes from that most excellent book:

1. "There is an aristocratic, self-indulgent holiness. It gives its influence to build up fine, costly houses of worship, with popular preachers, choir singing, select congregations, from which the poor are excluded as regular attendants, by selling or renting the seats. It puts on airs, dresses sufficiently in style to make the impression that it does not belong to the common people. It seeks the society of the upper classes, and endeavors to explain away the requirements of the gospel to suit their tastes. It goes as far in self-indulgence as public sentiment will permit.

2. "There is a fanatical holiness. It lays the greatest stress upon that which has the least reason and scripture for its support. Its self-denial is great, and is only equalled by its self-will. It has in it an element of sincerity, but it is vitiated by being consecrated to its own will rather than to the will of God. It lacks the great quality of submission. It does not know how to yield, even in matters the smallest and most indifferent. It must have its own way in everything. Everyone must submit to its dictation or receive its fiery denunciation.

3. "There is a covetous holiness. It wears cheap clothing,

but it is to avoid expense. It has a sharp criticism for every project that calls for an expenditure of money; but it is because it is unwilling to bear its part. It may have little, or it may have much, but what it has it holds onto with a miser's grasp. It is mighty in tearing down— it never tries its hand at building up. It may burn palaces— it cannot rear a hovel.

4. "Much of the current holiness is wanting in spirituality. It has a worldly aspect. Generally it talks after a worldly manner. It keeps up a profession of holiness where it is popular to profess holiness. But in general its conversation is of the earth, earthy. It lacks the odor of sanctity. It does not bear the solemn, heavenly aspect of one who holds communion with God. Notwithstanding its efforts to the contrary, it carries with it and diffuses wherever it goes a worldly spirit.

5. "If selling or renting pews in houses of worship is a plain violation of the prohibition to have respect of persons in seating congregations, and is contrary to the spirit and teaching of the gospel, then that holiness is defective which gives its sanction or support to this anti-Christian practice.

6. "If the Bible requires plainness of dress and forbids Christians to adorn themselves with braided hair or gold or pearls or costly array, then is that holiness defective which pays no attention to these plain commands, but conforms to the fashions of the world in things plainly forbidden by the word of God." J.T.L.

24
ADVICE TO THOSE PROFESSING HOLINESS

THE LIFE OF PERFECT LOVE is the ideal earthly life. Peaceful in all its relations, perfectly adjusted in all its operations, and lofty in all its aspirations, it is a life well calculated to win the admiration of the unprejudiced unbeliever, and to delight the soul of him who realizes that in its possession he experiences daily within him the power of an endless life.

To those who have entered into the holiest by the blood of Jesus, the writer would make the following suggestions:

1. *Cherish the thought of an indwelling Christ.* Our divine Lord has said, "Lo! I am with you alway, even unto the end of the world." The burden of the testimony and of the prayer of God's people so often indicates that Christ is afar off, and that the heart is longing for his presence. This is not as Christ would have it. His conception of right spiritual relation is that of an indwelling Lord holding communion with the redeemed spirit. He is there to control every appetite, to keep every passion in willing subjection unto himself, to guide every volition into legitimate channels of action, and to regulate every power and function of

the soul. Then give yourselves over to him to be "kept by the power of God, through faith, unto salvation."

2. *Let the Holy Ghost be your cherished teacher.* When pride and arrogancy have been brought low and destroyed, when all self-sufficiency and vain-glorious boasting have ceased, there is sure to exist in the sanctified heart an insatiable longing to know the deep things of God.

The Master knew that this would be so. He knew how paltry and trivial all life's lighter pleasures would appear, how shadowy and unreal all its enticing art, how empty its vain and subtle logic, how unsatisfactory its deepest research after truth. As he looked into the faces of his chosen twelve, and realized that he must soon leave them alone, with no sympathy from earthly sources, he spoke these words of deepest significance, "But the Comforter, which is the Holy Ghost, whom the Father will send in my name, he shall teach you all things and bring all things to your remembrance, whatsoever I have said unto you." The Eternal Spirit, who came in accordance with that promise, filled all their lives with highest thought, and thrilled their souls with revelations of an unseen world. Well did the apostles realize what wonderful compensation the Holy Spirit had made for all they had lost, for all they had suffered.

The apostle, in speaking of the things unseen by mortal eye and uncomprehended by the unregenerate mind, exclaimed, "But God hath revealed them unto us by his Spirit; for the Spirit searcheth all things, yea, the deep things of God."

This Searcher of the deep things of God, who is able to comprehend the mysteries of the universe about us, who understands perfectly all its laws and in just what relation each part should stand to the other; he, the Holy Ghost, has been designated as the Teacher of the saints.

The Holy Spirit, perchance, may have led many of the saints who read these lines to give up the cherished ambitions of their lives. Some would have devoted themselves to art, some to music, others to sculpture or painting. But God needed their heroism, their energy, their love, in places where these cherished projects of life could not be carried out. And so for love of Christ they have left chisel and brush and instrument and book, to serve in lowly places. Precious soul, if you have made such a sacrifice in love, the great teacher within you will surely give you glorious compensation. Does your nature long for harmony and song? What can excel the exquisite sweetness of that harmony which pervades the sanctified soul? And when the Holy Spirit strikes with skilful touch the chords of our sanctified passions, the harmony swells, until the soul bursts into a song of lofty praise, a song that opera or drawing room never heard, that old, old song of Moses and the Lamb. Have you longed to trace the landscape or portray the human form? The Holy Spirit is a subjective artist. He can make your soul all glorious within and hang all its walls with pictures and portraits of spiritual beauty. In hours of pious meditation retire within your own soul, and there behold the portrayals of the Holy Spirit. There is the figure of your dying Lord. Gaze upon him and think once more of his suffering, his self-denial, his tender love; think of what he has been to you and what his love has still in store, and as you meditate upon these things with moistened eye and subdued spirit, you will doubtless say that never form or figure moved you as do these revelations of your dying Lord.

The heavenly mansions and houses made without hands are specimens of spiritual architecture. Thoughts that leap beyond the reach of telescopic vision are the sparks of spiritual inspiration. No shallow eloquence, no fallacies of thought, no tricks of logic in the great Teacher's language.

He is the *truth*. Does your heart long for wisdom? One moment of silent communion with him has often given to the soul of man revelations of truth that the investigations of years have not furnished. Let him guide you into *all truth.*

3. *Let divine love have full sway in your lives.* Love is neither narrow, nor ascetic, nor inert. It is rather of such a nature that its very presence is recognized by the dynamic force it lends to action. That force is not directed into narrow channels, so that it is tumultuous, fitful, and destructive, but its might is exerted mildly, constantly, and beneficently. It gives warmth to the affections, stimulates the intellect, gives polish to thought, fires the imagination, quickens the memory, energizes the will, and kindles the altar fires of worship. It looks forth from the eye, spiritualizes the countenance, dignifies the carriage, and frees the voice from "tones of earthly passion."

This love our Lord has given to be the regulator of our earthly lives. If it be given full sway, it will render any life free from "spot, or wrinkle, or any such thing."

ALBERT H. STILWELL, A.M.,
Professor of Latin and Philosophy, Greenville College

Holiness at Death

I was happily converted,—
    'Twas many years ago,—
But soon after, I remember,
    I felt an inward foe.
This to me was quite surprising—
    I wondered what it meant;
To learn about the matter, to
    My minister I went.

He told me that I must endure
    And fight these foes through life;
And grim death at last would come
    And end the inward strife.
That sometimes they would trip me up,
    And then I must repent;
That I amid these ups and downs
    Must keep a good intent.

This made me sad; and yet I thought
    A preacher ought to know,
And fully there made up my mind
    To fight the life-time foe;
My only hope of holiness
    Was on the boundary line—
This side of vast eternity—
    Just at the close of time.

Yet my heart had love for Jesus,
    Hated each foe within,
And I often found it longing
    To be made free from sin.
Oft 'twould rise above my theory;
    In spite of it would pray,
"Blessed Jesus! my Redeemer!
    Oh, take these stains away!"

Would not the Lord be mocking me,
    Thus to beget a prayer,
And yet make it impossible
    To get an answer here?
No author of confusion, he
    Has ordered things aright;
My heart and head did not agree—
    A most unpleasant plight.

And then I found within myself
    A human love for life,
By intuition God had taught
    With death to have a strife.
And yet the Lord had caused my heart
    To long with every breath
For what my theory always taught
    Was only found in death.

My love for life and heart's desire
    At times would both be strong;
A stubborn fact before me stood—
    God or my theory's wrong.
Would he in nature raise a cry
    Against my heart's desire,
And yet within my heart a prayer
    For holiness inspire?

Then I read about old Enoch:
    Paul said, he pleased the Lord;
Three hundred years of victory,
    Then went to his reward.
He did not die— God took him;
    But did he go unclean?
Or did the Lord for him renounce
    Part of redemption's scheme?

And I read about Elijah,
    Who took a wondrous ride
Straight to heaven in a chariot;—
    That pilgrim never died.
He on earth was made white-hearted,
    And surely went up pure;
Otherwise the holy angels
    Could not the sight endure.

While looking up the promises,
    My doctrine to sustain,
I found them in the present tense,—
    This made my theory lame;
For not one word in them was found
    About a future time;
In every one 'twas plainly seen
    The blessing now was mine.

So then I turned to the commands,
    To see if they agreed;
And, lo, with promises they stood,
    To fill a present need;
For, "Be ye perfect", clear as light
    Flamed from the sacred page:
If God requires now, why should I
    Wait for a half an age?

As thus I read the holy word,
    It filled me with alarm;
No death-redemption promised there—
    My theory lost its charm.
I saw at once the fearful risk
    Of waiting until death;
Vanished all hopes of holiness
    Obtained with my last breath.

Thank God! at last my head was clear;
    This gave my heart a chance;
No longer by a dogma held,
    It made a bold advance.
Though some maintained it mattered not
    What anyone believed,
I found that my wrong view withheld
    What I should have received.

My heart broke out in strong desire
    To enter into rest;
And soon I felt the holy fire
    Flaming within my breast.
It went down to the very depths
    And purged out all my sin;
I found in life my Beulah land;
    By faith I entered in.

REV. S. K. WHEATLAKE,
Of the Ohio Conference

Out and Into

"He brought us out that he might bring us in."

Out of the distance and darkness so deep,
Out of the settled and perilous sleep,
Out of the region and shadow of death,
Out of its foul and pestilent breath,
Out of the bondage and wearying chains,
Out of companionship ever with stains;
    Into the light and glory of God,
    Into the holiest, made clean by the blood,
    Into his arms— the embrace and the kiss—
    Into the scene of ineffable bliss;
    Into the quiet, the infinite calm,
    Into the place of the song and the psalm.
Wonderful love that has wrought all for me!
Wonderful work that has thus set me free!
Wonderful ground upon which I have come!
Wonderful tenderness welcoming home!

Out of the horror at being alone,
Out, and forever, of being my own;
Out of the hardness of heart and of will,
Out of the longings which nothing could fill;
Out of the bitterness, madness and strife,
Out of myself and of all I called life;—
    Into communion with Father and Son,

    Into the sharing of all that Christ won;
    Into the ecstasies, full to the brim;
    Into the having of all things with him.
    Into Christ Jesus, there ever to dwell;
    Into more blessings than words e'er can tell.
Wonderful lowliness— draining my cup!
Wonderful purpose that can ne'er give me up!
Wonderful patience that waited so long:
Wonderful glory to which I belong!

Out of my poverty, into his wealth,
Out of my sickness, into pure health,
Out of the false, into the true.
Out of what measures the full depth of "Lost!"
Out of it all— but at infinite cost!
    Into what must with the cost correspond,
    Into that which there is nothing beyond.
    Into the union which nothing can part,
    Into what fills every want of my heart.
    Into the deepest of joys ever had—
    Into the gladness of making God glad.
Wonderful Person, whose face I behold!
Wonderful story, then all to be told!
Wonderful all the dread way that he trod!
Wonderful end— he has brought me to God!

—UNKNOWN

The Master's Touch

Matthew 8:15

"He touched her hand and the fever left her."
   He touched her hand as he only can,
With the wondrous skill of the Great Physician,
   With the tender touch of the Son of man;
And the fever pain in the throbbing temples
   Died out with the flush on brow and cheek,
And the lips that had been so parched and burning
   Trembled with thanks she could not speak.
And the eyes where the fever light had faded,
   Looked up, by her grateful tears made dim,
And she rose and ministered in her household,—
   She rose and ministered unto him.

"He touched her hand and the fever left her."
   Oh, we need his touch on our fevered hands!
The cool, still touch of the Man of sorrows,
   Who knows us, and loves us, and understands.
So many a life is one long fever!
   A fever of anxious suspense and care,
A fever of getting, a fever of fretting,
   A fever of hurrying here and there.
Oh! what if in winning the praise of others
   We miss at last the King's "Well done?"

If our self-taught tasks in the Master's vineyard
   Yield nothing but leaves at the set of sun?

"He touched her hand and the fever left her."
   Oh, blessed touch of the Man Divine!
So beautiful then to arise and serve him,
   When the fever has gone from your life and mine.
It may be the fever of restless serving,
   With the heart all thirsty for love and praise,
And eyes all aching and strained with yearning
   Tow'rd self-set goals in the future days.
Or it may be a fever of pain and anger,
   When the wounded spirit is hard to bear,
And only the Lord can draw forth the arrows
   Left carelessly, cruelly rankling there.

Whatever the fever, his touch can heal it;
   Whatever the tempest, his voice can still;
There is only joy as we seek his pleasure;
   There is only rest as we choose his will.
And some day, after life's fitful fever,
   I think we shall say, in the home on high,
'If the hands that he touched but did his bidding,
   How little it matters what else went by!'
Ah, Lord! thou knowest us altogether,
   Each heart's sore sickness, whatever it be;
Touch thou our hands! let the fever leave us,
   And so shall we minister unto thee.

            —Selected by Julia F. Holmes.

Members of Schmul's Wesleyan Book Club buy these outstanding books at 40% off the retail price.

Join Schmul's Wesleyan Book Club by calling toll-free:
800-S$_7$P$_7$B$_2$O$_6$O$_6$K$_5$S$_7$

Put a discount Christian bookstore in your own mailbox.

Visit us on the Internet at
www.wesleyanbooks.com

You may also order direct from the publisher by writing:
Schmul Publishing Company
PO Box 776
Nicholasville, KY 40340